IF YOU
ONLY KNEW...

CHAD VARGA
WITH LISA YODER

TO: THE MOORE'S,
Thanks For Everything!
Stay In Touch!

770.520.6211 Chad

Please note that Inspire's publishing style capitalizes certain pronouns in Scripture that refer to the Father, Son, and Holy Spirit, and may differ from some Bible publishers' styles.

Published by:
Inspire Communications, Inc.
P.O. Box 3003
Suwanee, GA 30024-0987
www.inspirenow.com

ISBN 0-9719-2640-9

DEDICATION

This book is dedicated to my best friend, my Lord and Savior Jesus Christ. You told me in Your word that You would never leave me nor forsake me, and You never have. Even when I felt like giving up and I thought no one was there – You were there. You are the author and finisher of my faith.

This book is also dedicated to my loving family: Kristie, my wife of almost ten years, and my incredible son and precious little girl, Cameron and Kiersten. You are more than my family; you are my life, and I love you more than words can express. My prayer for you is that you will have an undying love for Jesus Christ and that a passion for the lost will burn within you.

ENDORSEMENTS

"Inspiring… Chad's life is an incredible story of destiny and purpose… this book is a must read."

John C. Maxwell *Author, Speaker and Founder, The INJOY Group*

"Chad's life story is proof that success must be deserved. Throughout his life he has demonstrated an incredible ability to overcome obstacles in order to achieve his dreams."

Rick Pitino *Head Men's Basketball Coach, University of Louisville*

"Chad is a young man that always gave his best in pursuit of his goals. A winner is someone that gets the maximum out of their ability and that, my friends, is Chad Varga."

Dick Vitale *ESPN / ABC College Basketball Analyst*

"Every now and again a book appears on the shelves of bookstores that has the ability to captivate readers and change lives. *If You Only Knew…* is that book for today."

Chris Singleton *Oakland A's #2*

"Every generation needs heroes. Chad Varga has been through the pain of this generation. He speaks to the hurt and the hope of this generation."

Billy Joe Daugherty *Senior Pastor, Victory Christian Center, Tulsa, OK*

"Chad's life is a story in which people who are the most hurting can find hope. This book is a miracle. So is Chad."

Dave Roever *Founder and President, Roever Evangelistic Association*

"Chad's story is one that truly embodies my favorite quote from Jim Elliott, 'He is no fool who gives what he cannot keep, to gain what he cannot lose.' Chad's honesty and willingness to be obedient will impact the lives of many."

Jeanne Mayo *Jeanne Mayo Ministries, Rockford, IL*

"Chad's life is an example of overcoming adversity with perseverance, commitment, and hard work. This book reveals Chad's infectious enthusiasm and will speak loudly in the life of the reader."

Tom Crean *Head Men's Basketball Coach, Marquette University*

"Here's a true story of one kid's determination to defeat his enemy... average! I know it's true because he and I lived much of this together. This book will inspire the reader to maintain a strong faith in God, and realize that with Him, the impossible can become possible. Never will you find a person with Chad's intensity, zeal and pure determination. It made him great in basketball, and even greater in life."

Tim Bach *Youth Pastor, Griffin First Assembly of God, Griffin, GA*

"An awesome book that this hurting and hopeless generation can relate to and find hope in. I highly recommend this book."

Richard Crisco *Pastor of Student Ministries, Brownsville Assembly of God*

"This millennial generation is searching for real and genuine role models who understand their hurt, pain and fear. Chad doesn't just write about it, he lived it and has found great purpose through it. This book will give many hope and a determination to let nothing keep them from the greatness God desires and has designed for them."

Danny Chambers *Senior Pastor, The Oasis Church, Nashville, TN*

"The harder the battle, the sweeter the victory. Chad has wrestled with life and won a surpassing victory that will affect the eternal destiny of millions."

J. Paul Furrow
Senior Pastor, Colonial Heights Assembly of God, Colonial Heights, VA

"A powerful book that will confront, challenge, and inspire you to reach for your destiny in God."

Tony Brock *Senior Pastor, Hope and Life Fellowship, Snellville, GA*

"I am struck with a real sense of grief and alarm in reading this astonishing story. But even more, I am overwhelmed by the gut wrenching faith, passion and trust that was instilled in a young boy. This is a real-life-story of victory, that has and will continue to jar free hurting people through the power of God. Chad's story touches hearts while laying before us the despondency of a generation in desperate need of the real Jesus."

Jeff Deyo Recording Artist / Formerly of SONICFLOOd

"Easy reading and hard hitting… an amazing story of God's fulfilled purpose in a life!"

Darius Johnston *Senior Pastor, Christ Church, Fort Worth, TX*

"Chad's book is fresh and inviting. Each chapter leads you to read the next. It's a portrait of Almighty God at work in the life of a surrendered servant."

Jeff Appling *Senior Pastor, Grove Level Baptist, Maysville, GA*

"Chad is a man whose message is anointed and on target."

Jentezen Franklin *Senior Pastor, Free Chapel Worship Center, Gainesville, GA*

CONTENTS

FOREWORD

Sometimes the universe experiences a phenomenon known as a quasar, which is a star-like object that is an immensely powerful source of light. Not without occasion, but certainly infrequently, so also there are times when people explode on the scene with brilliance, bringing with them the uniqueness of a gift not found in the "solar system" of current experience. In the following pages the reader will find, in Chad Varga's first attempt at pulling scabs off still-healing wounds, that some bleeding will be revealed. His heart for kids screams through in an almost surreal story, but the sad truth is just that... it is the truth. The beginning of his training to be a premier speaker is traced to the trouble he found in childhood. The pressure of adolescence forced on him subsequent years that only served to make the pages of this book even more relevant to today's generation.

I will never forget the day my phone rang with Chad Varga on the other end asking to be mentored. My health was at an all-time low since the days of my horrific injuries in Vietnam. I wanted to say "No," but the heart of Chad was too much to deny. It seemed too much to ask – not on my part... but on his. He would have to walk away from more money from basketball contracts than I could imagine. I never thought he would do it. A quasar hit the night sky with brilliance. His story of suffering and salvation is the light thousands of students are seeing on campuses across America today. I have mentored many young people over the years, but Chad Varga stands out as the fastest learner with the biggest heart, and a story in which people who are the most hurting can find hope. This book is a miracle. So is Chad.

Dave Roever

Founder and President, Roever Evangelistic Association

CHAPTER 1

FACING THE FIGHT WITHIN

Squinting against the bright sun, I swung the bag of gear over my shoulder as I walked home from basketball practice. Coach was especially demanding that day. Even though I felt dead tired, an exhilarated feeling flowed through my muscles from the late afternoon workout. As I rounded our street corner, something caused me to pull up short, and I felt a cold chill race through my body.

I sprinted to the front door and threw it open. Two faces turned toward me in surprise as the door slammed hard against the frame. The sight before me grew ugly as my eyes adjusted to the dim light of the living room – standing frozen momentarily were my mom and her boyfriend, his one arm forcing her against the wall while the other drew back in a clenched fist.

With a sneer of disgust shot my way, he immediately resumed action as his fist slammed into Mom's face and she slid to the floor. Throwing the bag off and bringing my right arm back in one motion, I hit the boyfriend square on the jaw.

He punched me in the stomach and I dropped to my knees. Grabbing his leg, I threw him to the floor. Reaching out for a nearby lamp, I smashed it against the side of his head.

Then he unleashed his full force against me.

Taking me to the ground again, he beat me down forcing me into a position that kept me from moving. He dragged me to my room and threw me on the bed, swearing death over me the whole time. I wondered if this was going to be another one of those all night recurring episodes of fight round after fight round.

I rolled over onto my side, gasping for breath. Fists still clenched, I eyed the door - tense, ready, waiting for him to burst back through it. I carefully licked the blood from my lower lip. Still drawing deep breaths, I cried out to myself, "What's the point?" I decided, "It's time to just give up. Life has no purpose for me; I'm a nobody. Nobody cares." There I was at 14 years old, having to literally fight day in and day out; exhausted with life, I was at a breaking point.

"Why does life have to be so hard?" I asked through hot tears that streamed angrily down onto the sheets. "Why is life so *unfair?* No one will miss me if I just check out on life. No one cares what I'm goin' through. No one has ever cared," I said to myself. To prove my point, I thought back to my early childhood.

We were rushing along in the car toward home. Agitated, Mom was snapping angrily at us as she dragged my sister and me into the apartment. I was just under two years old and Wendy was almost four.

Pushing Wendy into the closet, Mom popped the lock and turned to me. "Look at you!" she ranted. "You're filthy! Can't you ever stay out of the dirt?" She yanked me up by the arms and headed for the bathroom. Flipping on the bathroom light, she began to strip my clothes off. She became more and more incoherent as she talked about how dirty I was and how I needed a bath.

"Get clean," she demanded, twisting the faucet on full force and throwing me down into the tub, hurting me.

As she left the room, I began to feel the rushing water filling up around me. Then I started to sense the water's temperature; it was scalding hot. Strung out on drugs, she had turned only the hot water on full force. Struck with sudden terror, I jumped up on the tub's edges with my hands and feet pushed against the wall to stay out of the water. Just a toddler, I was frozen with panic.

The water continued to rise toward me. Mom was clueless; she was passed out in her bedroom. Blistering water filled the tub and began to overflow, burning my feet. I stayed pushed against the tub walls for hours, not knowing how to get down without burning my whole body.

Across town, an aunt suddenly became heavily burdened for my sister Wendy and me. Racing to our apartment, she tried to get in. The doors were locked and Mom couldn't be roused. Our aunt looked into our bedroom and saw we weren't there. Then, she looked into Mom's room and saw her passed out on the floor.

Frantically, she broke a window. Hearing the water, she rushed to me in the bathtub and lifted my naked little body out of danger. She found Wendy, wrapped me up and took us home with her, where she cared for my burned feet.

"O.K., so God moved on my aunt's heart to rescue us," I conceded to myself. That was the first sign of the involvement of a living God in my life. "I guess I can't use that incident as evidence in my case of how no one ever cared for me because God did show up and act on my behalf," I admitted almost sullenly.

"What about all the other times?" I reminded myself angrily as I thought back to the frequent, terror-filled car rides with Mom. "Who cared then?"

CHAPTER 2

HIDING FROM THE POLICE

Mom, Wendy and I came out of the convenience store. Still a toddler, I had to hurry to keep up as we walked across the parking lot to the car. Neither Wendy nor I knew Mom was high though. Wendy climbed in the back and I in the front.

The instant the engine turned over, Mom floored the accelerator and began a familiar tirade. "You don't love me!" she screamed at us both as the car sped faster and faster down the road. Careening along, she opened her door, acting like she was going to jump, threatening us with, "Everything will be better if I'm dead."

Fearful and frightened, I began to yell at Mom to stop, which only infuriated her further. She snapped her right arm up to her chest and came back full force with her open hand across my face. Blood began to pour from a deep split in my lip.

Suddenly, she spotted a police car and became alarmed. Turning down a back road, she pulled into a driveway. Holding my hand to my lip, she pushed me down to the floorboard and yelled for both Wendy and me to hide. Scared, bleeding and crying, I huddled to the floor as she hissed warnings to us about the danger of the policeman finding us. We stayed in that driveway for a long time before Mom finally calmed down enough to realize I needed medical attention.

One might assume that most preschoolers would love the freedom to do whatever they wanted. For Wendy and me though, it only meant fear and insecurity when Mom frequently took us to her boyfriend's house. There, Mom and her boyfriend would party and do unspeakable things while Wendy and I were free to wander in and out of the house. We often played in the back yard near the pool. One day I tottered over to the clear blue water and reached over to pull something out of the pool; instead I found myself plunging through the water.

Quickly, I sank to the bottom and began gasping, surprised to find that instead of air, water was pouring into my lungs. I sucked in more and more water as I began to drown.

My fall didn't go unnoticed by Wendy, who carefully lowered herself into the shallow end where I lay at the bottom. She reached under the water and was able to clasp my pant's waistband and pull me out of the pool.

Laying me on the ground, Wendy pounded on my chest until water began to gush from my mouth and I started gasping air instead of water. Color returned to my blue lips as oxygen went back into my little body.

Reflecting back on that incident, my bedroom was turning dark with the fall of evening. I was tense wondering if I'd be up fighting all night. However, I was willing to concede that Wendy was watching out for me then. "Even so, it shouldn't have been my four-year-old sister who had to play the role of the mom for me," I thought to myself as hot tears returned. "Besides, sometimes Wendy couldn't protect even herself." I remembered many terrifying nights after Mom and Dad divorced and she had custody of us.

CHAPTER 3

ANOTHER NIGHT OF TERROR

In a deep sleep, I was breathing regularly. Suddenly I was yanked from bed and ordered out of the house with Wendy. It was two a.m. and neither Wendy nor I knew where Mom was taking us this time.

Mom sped through the dark, empty streets toward the downriver, Woodhaven area of Detroit. Screeching to halt, she parked the car next to a broken out street lamp and barked at us to get out of the car. Grasping Wendy's arm in one hand and mine in the other, she dragged us up the dingy, crack house staircase.

Still sleepy, Wendy and I hardly noticed the drug addicts and dealers we passed along the way. Coming to a room with an old wooden door with only traces of cracked paint still clinging to it, Mom jerked it open and threw us into the room.

Landing on the gritty floor, Wendy and I crawled through the dirt to a cold corner of the room. I could feel Wendy's four-year-old body tremble as she pulled me close. Her brown hair brushed against my cheek as our eyes adjusted to the smoky room.

Looking across the room, we noticed a longhaired man sitting near the door with skintight jeans and a tie-dyed shirt. He was staring hard at us with a crazed look in his eye. Close up against his chin he was holding a small handgun.

We had no idea why we were there, why the man had a gun or what was going to happen to us. Wendy brought her quivering lips close to my ear and began to whisper softly, "Jesus keep us safe."

"Jesus keep us safe," I joined her.

Quietly, we pressed close and spent the next couple of hours praying that one, four-word prayer. Finally the door eased open; having had her fix, Mom was ready to go home. We never found out why the man had a gun.

Just like so many other nights after visiting different crack houses in various parts of the city, Wendy and I climbed back into bed just before daybreak and tried to sleep. We were often so overcome with exhaustion, we couldn't do anything but lay awake waiting for morning to come.

We were too young to know how to explain to anyone what was happening to us. Since my mother had been granted custody, not even Dad was aware of the terrifying days and nights we were spending with Mom. Mom blamed us for her behavior.

One of four daughters, she had grown up in church. Her own mother, a fantastic prayer warrior who loved God with all her heart, would take the girls to different church events where they would sing. Beautiful and talented, they were always well received.

Mom grew up in the Detroit area and surrounding suburbs, where she met my father at the Mamre Assembly of God Church as a teenager. They fell for each other and married young. I suppose it was a form of escape as well as love for both of them.

My mother's home wasn't all peace; her father was a violent alcoholic. She grew up between the extremes of a Godly mother who had found the Lord during her girl's childhood years and an alcoholic father.

Her mother would walk the girls over a mile to church and back twice on Sunday and every Wednesday. Her mother's life was immediately changed, from a life of despair to a future full of hope. She committed her life fully to God, in spite of her husband's actions. It was her father's addictive personality though that Mom took hold of for her own life.

My father was escaping from a home life bound in mental depression. When Dad met Mom, he knew she was the woman, and the only woman, for him. Mom was beautiful, talented and full of all the potential in the world. He thought everything was great once they married.

It didn't take long though for him to begin to discover the other side of Mom – the life she lived away from church. He had been totally unaware of her partying, the drugs she experimented with in high school or the addictive personality she hid. When she went out on him just six months after their marriage, he was blindsided. Despite his deep hurt, he decided to reconcile.

My sister Wendy was born soon afterwards, and things were good for a while. Soon after my birth, Mom began partying and going to bars again – she became obsessed with doing her own thing.

Every day of our lives, Dad got Wendy and I down on the floor to pray. Mom would be out cheating on him, but he always believed God was going to touch his wife. He saw the potential in her and believed that some day, some how, some way, she would come back to God. God would restore her and she would make it. He knew Christ would accept her, and she would become the mom she was capable of being.

Dad knew the things Mom was involved in were happening because the devil was fighting for her life. Satan was trying not only to destroy her, but take us all with her, and my father was determined not to let the enemy win.

Finally, just before I turned three, my father and mother divorced. The whole family thought it was obvious that Dad would get custody. The courts however, only considered a mother as a primary caregiver and nurturer. Mom was sharp too; she won custody. It was during those years while Dad continued to seek custody that our lives were the most unpredictable. Mom would often try to lay the blame of the upheaval in our family squarely on my father's shoulders.

Still huddled on my bed as darkness fell, I thought back to that traumatic day in Wyandotte, Michigan.

CHAPTER 4

A SISTER'S PRAYER

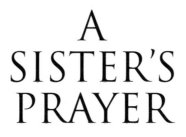

I was four years old, and we were all coming home in the car. Mom had come back with us for a while. Dad was praying it would work out, but Mom was heavily into cocaine and alcohol again. Dad was driving, and Mom was in the passenger seat strung out. Wendy and I were in the backseat. Mom was trying to egg Dad on.

Hallucinating, Mom grabbed the seatbelt and wrapped it around her neck telling us kids in the backseat, "Look! Your dad is choking me!" Even at our young ages of four and six, we could see clearly she was doing it herself.

The car pulled into the driveway, and no sooner had Dad shifted into park, than Mom grabbed the keys from the ignition. As we were getting out of the backseat, she took her cigarette and burned Dad on the leg, still trying to pull him into a fight.

Just a little guy, I couldn't see what was happening in the car, but Wendy could. She peered through the front window as Mom took the keys, held them up to her mouth and pulled them hard across her gums. Flying out of the front seat with blood gushing from her mouth, she looked at Wendy and me and said, "Look! Look what your dad did! This is why I do what I do."

Wendy responded pleadingly, "No, Mom. I saw what you did with the keys."

That immediately sent Mom into a fit of rage. Dragging Wendy up the stairs of our duplex, she continued to rant at Dad, hitting and pounding on him. The fight against Dad escalated. From just outside the room, I watched as dishes smashed against the wall and glass flew everywhere, onto counters, into the sink and across the floor and table.

Picking up a heavy dining room chair, Mom rushed past Dad and shattered the second floor window. She continued to wildly slam the chair into the window to break out all the glass and much of the frame. Drywall cracked off in hunks as puffs of plaster and dirt sprayed out into the air. Dad grabbed her by the arm as she began crawling out. "Let go of me!" she screamed.

Shaking with fear, I watched as she tried to jump from the window. Just then, six-year-old Wendy gripped my arm firmly and led me back into what we called the cold room because of the overwhelming blue walls and ceiling.

Shouts and screams filtered back to us as Dad carried on the struggle with Mom. Seized with alarm that Mom was going to kill herself, Wendy pulled me to floor, crying and frightened herself. Wendy knelt, her green eyes wet with tears, and said to me, "We need to pray." She prayed a prayer that stayed with me the rest of my life, "God," she said taking a deep breath, "I don't know why our family is going through this. But I know that you have a purpose for my life and for Chad's life."

"Purpose! Ha!" I said bitterly to myself. "I didn't even know the meaning of the word then at the age of four. I'm 14 now and what purpose has there been in my life?" I said to myself, biting my lip and flinching with the suddenness of the sharp pain from where it was split.

As I reached up to tenderly feel the area of my left eye that was now swollen shut, one of my most traumatic memories came flooding back before I could stop it.

CHAPTER 5

"MOM, DON'T DIE!"

Mom was living in Brownstown Township, Michigan, just down the street from my grandmother, her mother. Wendy and I were visiting Mom and we were in the bedroom with her. Mom had been using drugs heavily lately, and this night was no exception.

Mom was sitting on the knotted bedspread, legs crossed. Her normally beautiful, sweeping hair was tangled, and there was a desperate look to her drawn face. She pulled a lighter from her faded jeans pocket. She concentrated hard on her quivering hand as she tried to place the rock of crack cocaine in the spoon held by her other unsteady hand.

She fumbled with the lighter until a bright flame appeared and began to heat the rock. Aware of what she was about to do, Wendy leapt onto the bed, and her green eyes clouded as she began to plead, "Mom, please! Don't!" she cried out in a voice that sounded more like a mother to an irresponsible child than of a six-year-old to her mom.

As if in slow motion, I watched the bed mattress give to Wendy's weight and then come back with a jolt. I saw Mom startle. I heard Wendy's pleas as if they were echos in a far away chamber. Then two tiny drops of liquid cocaine rolled over the spoon's edge and fell slowly like a miniature waterfall down, down onto the little white knots of the bedspread.

All in one instant, I saw Mom's fist clench and arm recoil in one sweeping motion as she slammed her fist into Wendy's mouth. Wendy flew to the floor whimpering as blood began to pour from where her tooth had gone through her lip. Panicked by Wendy's reaction, I began to scream, "Mom! Don't do this! Don't do this! Stop!"

Only further infuriated and more desperate, Mom threw me to the floor. I saw the track marks along her arm as she reached down toward me to grab my belt. With one hard yank, she whipped the belt out of its loops as I lay trembling next to Wendy. I scooted closer to Wendy as Mom, breathing heavily, finished heating the crack. She drew the belt tight around her upper arm and notched it firmly. Frantically looking for a vein, she took the needle of now liquid cocaine and shot it forcefully into her arm.

Instead of falling back into a deep trance as usual, Wendy and I watched in horror as her eyes rolled back in her head and she collapsed. Rolling from the bed with a resounding thud onto the wood floor, she lay in a crumpled heap. Wendy and I ran to her and began shaking her unresponsive body. "Mom! Mom! Are you O.K.?"

We had seen Mom high often enough to know this wasn't a normal trip. As the alarm rose in Wendy's voice, I struggled to understand what was happening. Somehow I knew I was losing my mom.

Wendy left me pounding on Mom and calling out to her as she rushed to the telephone to dial my grandmother's number, long memorized. Dad and Grandma had trained us to call them when anything happened with Mom.

"Grandma!" Wendy said frantically as tears began to well up in her throat, "Mom did drugs and passed out, but something's different. She won't answer us. She's not moving!"

Grandma reassured Wendy and then quickly called the emergency *squad housed just down the street. Within minutes, medical personnel and police flooded into the house. I watched someone pick up Wendy and carry her away, wiping the blood and tears from her face.*

A man gripped my arm tightly as he led me out of the way, but my eyes were glued to my mother. He took my face in his rough hands and turned it toward him as he began to question me. I didn't even know what he was saying because my ears were filled with the paramedics' voices, "She's unresponsive. There's no pulse. There's no heartbeat."

I turned back and looked down the endlessly long hallway into the bedroom where my mother lay dead and heard over and over, "There's no pulse," as they tried different things to revive her. They worked and worked on her there on the floor.

I couldn't even cry because I was so much in shock. I felt my own heart pounding wildly against my little chest as if it was going to burst as I heard them say again, "There's no heartbeat."

"She's gone."

I was too young to know that a person is usually brain dead after being flat-lined for six minutes. I was too young to be aware she'd been flat-lined for as long as an estimated seven minutes. I just wanted them to keep trying. I didn't want to lose my mother.

I hadn't given the man one answer. He began to lead me away, and then I heard, "We've got a pulse!" Things happened faster. They loaded Mom up onto a gurney with wires and tubes connected everywhere and rushed past us out of the house to the ambulance.

Two days later, I was back in my assigned seat in kindergarten singing songs and learning ABC's.

Jesus didn't fail me, I admitted. And, He didn't fail Mom.

While she was dead, she had a life after death experience. She was at the bottom of a slick, grassy hill. She was climbing and crawling to the top toward a bright light. Distraught, she clawed her way up until she couldn't get any further. A tall, black, wrought iron fence blocked her from the light – from God.

She couldn't talk; her lips wouldn't move. She cried out to God in her mind, "God, please send me back! Please send me back!" She knew if she stayed on that side of death, she wouldn't be with God. Her pleas ricocheted off the air, never reaching God's ear.

Defeated, she dropped her head into her hands. Then she remembered. Her mom had always told her that God had promised her mom that all her babies would end up in Heaven! As soon as that thought entered her mind, she was snapped back to life. God gave her another chance.

With the next death I witnessed, no one came back to life.

CHAPTER 6

MURDER!

I hated it when I had to stay with Mom. I hated the sirens and shouting at the complex where she lived. Most of all, I hated the apartment's living room — especially Thursday through Sunday nights. Those were Mom's party nights. People poured in and out of the apartment those nights getting high, getting drunk.

Boyfriends thought it was cute to scoop their beer suds off for me. Soon they were putting hard liquor into Kool-Aid, trying to get me drunk. I didn't know if they just wanted to shut me up, or if they only wanted to see the effects that alcohol would have on a little boy, but it humiliated me.

I hated the living room.

One Saturday night, I stayed in my room lining up toy cars and trucks on the floor, making them crash into each other, but quietly to avoid drawing attention to myself. It was very, very late. Trucks soon became boring, so when I heard a loud commotion just outside my window, I raced to the blinds to peek out.

Two guys were fighting heavily already. From the shouts I gathered that the 19-year-old had brought the 22-year-old's sister home too late, and this big brother was furious.

Only fifteen to twenty feet from my window, I was mesmerized as I watched the older guy pummel the younger one into the ground, beating him mercilessly until he was nearly comatose. The older man, shoulders back, stood panting over the kid, his hot breath making white puffs in the cold, night air.

Finally, the 19-year-old struggled to his feet, his eye-swollen shut and blood pouring from where teeth were missing and cracked. He staggered and tried to walk away.

That's when I saw the other man reach into his pocket and take out a nine-millimeter pistol. He raised it slowly to the other's head, pressing it deliberately to his right temple. Without one moment's hesitation, he pulled the trigger. The whole side of the kid's already bludgeoned face blew off. I watched as blood and tissue spattered on the apartment walls, the sidewalk and his clothes. With a slow and sickening motion, his body jerked, then crumpled, hitting the ground and rolling off the curb.

I was frozen with terror. I hated what I was seeing, but no part of my body would move. My feet wouldn't run, my mouth wouldn't scream and worst of all, my eyes wouldn't close.

It wasn't anything like the pretty picture Hollywood wants to paint for us on TV shows where a body just slumps to the ground; I saw the very life leave his body.

I was still standing there frozen, looking through the blinds when the twenty-two year old spit on the kid and kicked him. I heard myself gasping and choking, trying to cry, but I still couldn't move.

I was still standing there when he went into his apartment and came back with a sawed-off shotgun. I watched as he raised it with a steady, determined aim and laid six more shots into the kid's body. With each round, the lifeless body jumped and writhed from the force.

Finally, the sound of sirens, shouts and bright lights brought me *back to a state where I could move. I inched back from the window. I was breathing convulsively. I wanted my father – but the courts had said he couldn't have me. I didn't even consider heading into the living room out of fear of further abuse.*

In shock, I wandered around my room. I looked at my cars and trucks still lying on the floor. I gave them a hard kick. I looked for something else to play with, something to take away what I'd just seen. Dazed, I couldn't find anything.

I thought about how I wished my father were there, and I remembered something he told me once. We'd been on a long car ride and I had kept asking, "Are we there yet? How much longer?"

Dad had told me, "Son, lay down and go to sleep. You'll wake up and we'll be there. Time flies when you go to sleep."

"That's it!" I thought. I jumped into my bed and pulled my NBA sheets tight up around my neck. I concentrated with all my might to make my eyes shut.

It didn't work.

My eyes refused to close because they wouldn't look away from the window. I was convinced that the murderer was coming for me next. I expected him to break through the window with the sawed-off shotgun at any moment.

My heart raced as I tried to force myself to just go to sleep, but the terror and shock were all too real. Convinced no one at that apartment cared about me, I was a frightened little boy with no one to turn to. Nobody knew I was there or what had happened to me.

Finally, I took my eyes off the window and looked at the table next to my bed. Sitting on the table was my red, pictorial Bible. I loosened my hold on the sheets long enough to reach over and grab hold of it.

I clutched it to my chest and said aloud, "Jesus, give me peace." The reality of God, the reality of Jesus, flooded my room. A God who knew who I was, knew what I'd seen and cared met me in that moment.

My breathing steadied, and I continued whispering, "Jesus, give me peace." With each request, God brought comfort, peace and assurance to me. Within five minutes, I was sound asleep under the heavy, real presence of a living God who cares about little boys who are hurting deeply.

Now in my bedroom in Michigan I was hurting too – and not just from the bruises and scrapes of the evening's fight. The hurt was deep inside. The violence of my family had crept into my own life.

I wanted that same peace I had as a little boy huddled under my NBA sheets after seeing a gruesome murder. I wanted the peace that had allowed me to hold on to God firmly until now.

No, I didn't want to throw in the towel. I began to believe again in my sister's prayer; God did have a purpose for my life. I couldn't see any evidence of purpose, but I couldn't deny it either. No matter how miserable my situation was, God was real; I'd felt His very presence.

I reached across the bed of the now pitch-black room and fumbled with the nightstand drawer. Searching around with my hand, I finally took hold of a black, imitation leather, King James Bible.

I crawled under the sheets and clasped the Bible to my chest. Looking up to heaven, I whispered into the dark, "Jesus, give me peace."

CHAPTER 7

"HAPPY BIRTHDAY!"

Jesus did give me peace – the most precious kind of peace that exists – peace in the midst of turmoil and instability.

I had needed the peace of Jesus the year I turned eleven more than ever before. Mom had shown up where we were living in Cincinnati, and Dad had taken her back. Wendy remembers these years as the best our family ever had. Mom was holding down a job as well as Dad, and we had a nice home.

When Mom is doing well, she is phenomenal. She is beautiful, talented and the best cook in the world. She can plan and organize the greatest events. So, on the morning of my eleventh birthday, I burst out of bed with great expectations of the coming day.

I could smell the bacon and eggs as I raced down the stairs – no cold cereal today. It was my birthday!

At school my friends and I talked about the great time we were going to have that night. Mom had scheduled us to go to a big pizza place with all the games. Afterwards we would all head to our house, eat more food and all the guys were going to sleep over.

Finally, the school bell rang, and the guys and I headed for our house, playing and wrestling along the way. We tumbled loudly into the house. Immediately, I was aware it was too quiet. None of the guys noticed. The place was immaculate, the cake was set out on the table and a box waited to carry all the presents to the restaurant.

"Hello, Birthday Boy!" Wendy said, coming into the room and snapping a cardboard birthday hat on my head.

I leaned close to her ear and hissed in a near panic, "Where's Mom?"

Wendy's eyes darkened, "I don't know Chad. But, don't worry. Dad will be home in plenty of time to get us to the pizza place. Relax!" She pushed me into the living room where the guys had already started a Nintendo tournament.

I took Wendy's advice. Dad soon came through the door, and with all the commotion and excitement, I enjoyed the party. When we arrived back at the house, Dad succeeded in herding us all off to my room.

For the fourth time, the door to my bedroom swung open, "This is your last warning," Dad said, trying to sound stern. "No more talking! It's time to sleep." I was sure he could hear the muffled laughter as he walked down the hall.

Finally, everyone went to sleep - everyone but me. As I lay in the dark in my sleeping bag, the tears of disappointment came. I had so looked forward to celebrating my birthday as a family. I felt convinced nothing could make me feel more miserable. Then I heard the front door. My heart began to pound.

I leapt from my sleeping bag and vaulted over the bodies of my sleeping friends. Creeping down the stairs, I stopped at the living room doorway. I peeked around the corner to see Mom laid out across the couch. Certain that she was drunk and had forgotten about the party,

I tried to think of how to get her quietly off to bed without waking the whole house and causing a scene.

Noticing a big wad of money in her right hand, I could smell the alcohol before I even reached the couch, "Uh, hi, Ma."

"Oh," she said surprised someone was in the room with her, "Hi."

"Hey, Ma. Where'd you get the money? Were you playing craps? Wow, you must have been really good to win all that!"

"What?" she asked, confused, but I could tell by her reaction that the tone of voice I was using was working.

"Ma, I love you," I said taking her by the hand and helping her up. "You must be tired. Come on, you should go to bed."

"No, I'm not tired at all," she said getting louder.

I wondered if anyone upstairs could hear us. "Come on, Mom," I said, putting her arm around my shoulder. "That's right."

I coaxed her up the stairs and delivered her to the bedroom. Not even Dad woke up. I went back to my room and wove my way through sleeping bags full of bodies, relieved to see everyone still sound asleep.

Collapsing exhausted into my spot, I prayed for Mom like Dad had taught Wendy and I to do every day of our lives. Then I closed my eyes around my tears and breathed, "Jesus, give me peace," into the night air.

In my Michigan bedroom, now black with nightfall, I was still clutching the black, King James Bible as I remembered how Jesus answered those prayers for Mom in the most amazing of ways during an adventure to Atlanta.

CHAPTER 8

DAD'S ANGUISH

Dad cracked another joke and Wendy and I burst out into laughter again. Pulling lovingly on Wendy's hair, Dad teased her about her new haircut. She pushed him away playfully as we, loaded down with Taco Bell sacks, all tumbled into the house. We froze when we heard the soft music.

Like spectators watching a tennis match, our heads moved in unison as we swept our eyes over the spotless living room. We turned back toward the dining room and saw the table set for a gourmet meal. Delicious scents drifted from the kitchen. Defeated, we abandoned the taco bags on the table and dropped limply into chairs. We stared dumbly at one another.

We had all just moved back to Michigan from Cincinnati, Ohio, to be near our extended family again. "I'm sorry kids," Dad finally said, "I had no idea. I thought Mom was O.K. with the move." Dad had taken Mom back again; Dad always took Mom back whenever she showed any sign of getting better.

Wendy burst into tears and ran to her room. The past year or so had been the happiest family times she had ever had.

The signs were unmistakable: the clean house, the fabulous meal waiting and hot, the dim lights and music. It all meant only one thing — Mom had left. It was the way she always left. Instead of just walking out, she had an obsession to leave everything in perfect order, as if that somehow made up for the chaos her absences caused in our lives.

The uncertainty of it was hard on all of us. She could be gone a few weeks or a few months; we had no idea. We struggled through the first few weeks.

When it came time to pay the rent, more difficulties arose. Without Mom's income, there just wasn't enough to make it. I got tired of eating government-issued cereal, and I was fed up with substituting water for milk when I didn't want to eat it dry.

Dad came in late one night after working a double shift to make ends meet and found me rooting through the cupboards. "What are you looking for, son?" he asked as he laid down his jacket.

"Oh, nothing," I said giving him a typical 12-year-old answer, "I was just hungry for some chocolate." I went back to my television show.

A few minutes later, I heard the front door open and close and realized Dad had gone back out. "I wonder where he is going," I shrugged to myself.

The door opened a half-hour later, and Dad handed me a small brown sack from the Lawson's Dairy Mart, nearly a mile down the road, "I thought you might like this," he said.

I looked up at him surprised and opened the sack. Inside was a melting chocolate-coated, chocolate ice cream Klondike Bar. "Wow! Thanks Dad!" I jumped up and gave him a hug, realizing he must have gone into the bedroom and scraped together all the pennies and nickels he could find from the bottom of the dresser drawer to pay for the bar.

"You're welcome," he said, smiling down at me and ruffling my hair. He turned and headed to the bathroom for a shower.

Biting into the creamy chocolate, it was like I'd never tasted anything so good before. All my taste buds were on hyper-drive. I licked every sticky drop off the wrapper. Mom may not have wanted to be with us, but I knew Dad wouldn't be anyplace else in the world except with Wendy and I.

More weeks passed and we had to move out because we just couldn't afford the rent. At first we all moved in with Grandma Varga, but soon Wendy moved over to my Grandma Little's home instead. It was crowded at Grandma Varga's, and Grandma Little had just lost Grandpa and enjoyed having Wendy's company.

Dad and I shared a room at Grandma Varga's. I was startled awake one Saturday night four months after Mom left. It was three or four in the morning. "What is that sound?" I asked myself sleepily as I rubbed my eyes. I looked over to Dad's twin bed; it was him I heard.

He was sobbing uncontrollably. I leapt out of my bed and onto his. "Dad, what is it?" I asked alarmed.

"I don't know, son," he choked, "Your mom. Your mom. Something is happening with your mom."

I wrapped my arm around his shoulder, and he went back into deep prayer and intercession. We stayed that way for a long time. Finally he looked up at me.

"Chad, you know Mom left that muffled message on Grandma Little's answering machine last week saying something about Atlanta, right?" Dad asked giving me an uncertain look.

"Yeah, but that was it. We don't even know if she's really there. Besides, it's been months, Dad."

"I know, son," he gave me another uncertain look. "I know this sounds absolutely crazy. But, . . . I know the Holy Spirit is telling me to go to Atlanta and get your mom." He took me firmly by the shoulders,

"Somehow son, we have to go get your mom."

Now I gave him an uncertain look. "But Dad, we don't have any money. We don't even have a car," I said, my voice rising in unbelief.

"I know, son."

We both were quiet for a while.

"Atlanta sure is far away from Taylor, Michigan, isn't it," I said, making more of a statement than a question.

"Well, better get some sleep, son," Dad said as he pushed me toward my bed. "The Lord isn't going to give us such a strong burden without also giving us the means to carry it out."

Tucked in snug under the covers, I turned the thought over and over in my mind like I was examining a puzzle. "Go get Mom? In Atlanta?" The more I said it though, the less absurd it seemed.

Finally I heard Dad's steady breathing in the next bed, and I fell asleep too, wondering what the next day would bring.

CHAPTER 9

ATLANTA, HERE WE COME!

Someone was shaking me, hard.

"Son, son!"

Finally, I sat up in bed. "We overslept," Dad explained, "Better get ready quick. Church starts in half an hour."

Crawling out of bed, I stretched and wondered why I felt so tired. Then I remembered the night before, and I was wide-awake. I threw on my Sunday clothes, pushed my feet into my worn out penny loafers and raced to the kitchen where I grabbed a piece of toast as we headed out the door for church.

"How are we gonna do it, Dad?" I asked breathlessly.

"I don't quite know yet, Chad. I think I need to talk it over with Pastor after church though," he answered me thoughtfully.

The minute Children's Church was released, I was in the pew next to Dad anxious for the main service to end. It seemed like service took forever that Sunday. Finally, it was over.

I stayed in the pew and watched Dad head down the main aisle toward the pastor. Just before he reached him, a man in the second pew from the front stopped him. I saw him hand Dad an envelope and take his hand.

I rushed forward to hear what he was saying, "So Don, I want you to take this money and do what the Holy Spirit told you to do. There's two hundred dollars there. I don't know if that's all the money you need, but it's what the Holy Spirit told me to give you." He shook Dad's hand one more time, looked him in the eye and said, "Do what the Holy Spirit told you to do, Don."

Dad looked down at the envelope in wonder. He expressed his appreciation, and then continued toward the pastor. I went out front to the foyer to wait, anticipation rising in my spirit.

Soon an arm dropped across my shoulder, and Dad looked down at me, "Well, son, it means doing free lawn work all summer for your Grandmother's best friend, Francis, but we have the use of her car for the next three days."

"So, we're going?" I asked skeptically.

"Of course we're going," Dad smiled as we walked out of the church.

The cold stares slapped us in the face the moment we stepped out. Some of our extended family and friends were waiting for us. Somehow, word of Dad's plan to go to Atlanta had spread throughout the church.

"What are you doing, Don?" one aunt screeched.

"Are you out of your mind? After all the times Kathie has cheated and lied, what reason on earth could you have for wanting to bring her back?" another relative demanded.

"This must be the stupidest thing you have ever done Don, even worse than all the times you've taken Kathie back when she's come to you!" This relative threw up his hands in disgust, "But now you are actually going after her!"

"Yeah," several others chimed in, "Tell us Don; just tell us how you expect to find Kathie in a major city?"

I looked over helplessly at Dad. I couldn't believe he was just standing there, eyes down. "Why doesn't he say something?" I screamed inside my head.

"This is just another financial blunder, Don," an older relative said, pointing an accusing finger at the holes in my penny loafers, "Just look at Chad's shoes! Now that's what you better be using that money for."

I could feel the red rising to my face.

"Yes," another relative agreed, "and what about Wendy, Don? Did you stop to think of her? She needs clothes, Don – not her father going off on some wild goose chase!"

Finally I couldn't take the accusations any longer or Dad not fighting back. Fists clenching at my sides, I stood up tall and shouted, "Stop it! All of you just stop it!"

Other church members had been crowding around for some time now. I didn't care. "We have to go. You don't understand," I tried to explain, but I could see from the look on their faces, they felt only pity, not understanding.

"You don't know! You didn't see Dad last night on his face in prayer for hours - God speaking to him. God told him to go find Mom and, and we're gonna find her!" I looked around pleadingly for a sign that anyone understood. They all just shook their heads sadly as Dad led me to the borrowed car.

My father's hurt and pain were tangible in the very air as we slowly pulled the car doors shut. I watched Dad grasp the seat belt, pull it across his lap and lock it in place. He slumped back against the seat and passed his hand through his hair.

I could see the emotions passing across his face - hurt, grief and shame. Then I watched as the reality of the impossible task before us sank in, and hopelessness formed his features. It was like the echoes of my relatives' voices were in the car with us, and I could see them flowing across Dad's face.

"Are you crazy, Don?"

"You couldn't find Kathie in a little know-nothing town if she didn't want to be found."

"What makes you think she would come back, even if you could find her?"

"You can't find anyone in a city the size of Atlanta."

I saw Dad look down at my size 13 shoes and shake his head. He gave a deep sigh as he leaned back hard against the seat.

Then I saw the most amazing thing happen. All the blood that had drained from his face began to return, he squared his shoulders and I saw determination return to his clear, hazel eyes.

"Maybe there's more to being a man than defending yourself in a fight," I thought to myself as I watched this transformation take place.

He placed a strong arm on my shoulder, bowed his head and I heard him begin to pray with great confidence, "Father, I know what you told me to do. I know what you laid on my heart. It doesn't matter what they say; I'm going to obey your word to me."

He gave my shoulder a hard squeeze as he finished the prayer and turned, looking me in the eye, "Son, we're going to Atlanta!" The Pontiac 6000 roared to life, and we sped out of the church parking lot, heading due south.

CHAPTER 10

"MOM?"

I twisted off the lid of a Mountain Dew and handed it to Dad as we pulled out of the service station. Balancing the nachos and cheese on one knee and a sub sandwich on the other, I looked over at Dad. "God is so awesome!" I said excitedly.

"He sure is incredible, son," Dad answered back, reaching across to my shoulder with his free hand. I snuggled his arm between my shoulder and face like I'd done thousands of times growing up.

"Hand me my sandwich," Dad requested as we continued heading south.

"So, I'll miss at least one day of school too, huh, Dad?" I asked hopefully. He frowned at my enthusiasm, but we both knew he didn't mean it.

Lunch long over, we settled into quiet silence as Dad passed over the next state line. Both of us were wondering the same thing, "How can we possibly find Mom in a city the size of Atlanta?" Finally I dozed off in the seat.

Early Monday morning we continued our mission. We went from being pumped and full of faith, to wondering how we would even begin to look for, much less find, Mom. When discouragement mounted, Dad reached over and I snuggled his arm as he said, "Come on. We can do this, Chad. You just have to believe in what God told us, Faith is the evidence of things unseen."

Getting close to Atlanta, we took an exit off the highway. I started looking for a Wendy's so I could get a Frosty. Dad flipped off the radio, and silence filled the car. I looked at his face. He was staring intently across the road. I followed his gaze and leaned forward to see better. I saw a lady wearing a light blue shirt and cutoff jean shorts, her bleached-blond hair flying as she ran down the side of the road. Dad and I looked at one another dumbfounded and said in unison, "Mom?"

Dad spun the car around. We were whooping and hollering. Dad pulled up behind her. I jumped out of the car and took off running. "Mom!" I screamed. "Mom! It's Chad, stop!"

A thousand thoughts assaulted my mind in an instant when she didn't stop right away. "Maybe my uncle was right; she doesn't want to be found." "How stupid could you be Chad, thinking she'd want to come back with you?" and "She doesn't care about you; she isn't going to stop."

I ran faster and harder, the tears starting to sting my face in the wind. "Mom!" I cried out again, "Please stop!"

She turned at the sound of my voice and peered suspiciously over her shoulder. When she saw it was me, she came running, arms open wide. Then she spotted Dad and we collapsed together in a heap there beside the road, crying and hugging.

Dad headed for the nearest restaurant, where he had a long talk with Mom about coming home with us. She agreed.

Much later we found out some of what was happening to her in Atlanta.

She had hitchhiked out of Michigan when she left us in October. She was headed for Florida when this guy from Georgia picked her up. He was running a crack house outside Atlanta and convinced Mom to join him for a fix. Before she realized what was happening, she was trapped in a relationship with him, surrounded by other dangerous people in the drug world. Besides drugs, he provided her with plenty of violence and abuse.

Befriended by one of the guy's friends, Mom was informed one night that he had grown tired of her. He was going to kill her. "You can get out if you go now," the friend warned.

Sneaking out of the house, Mom took off running at full-speed and didn't stop until nearly three miles later when she heard her son calling to her along an expressway just outside Atlanta.

Mom agreed to come back to Michigan, but she didn't come home to live with us that time. She went into rehabilitation instead. I had to move to a new school – again. It was there that I found out something about myself for the first time.

CHAPTER 11

A NEW DISCOVERY

My heart sank when I realized that for the fourteenth time, I was going to be the new kid in school. Dad had taken a construction position in North Carolina in the middle of my eighth grade year. Mom was doing well in rehabilitation and had stayed behind in Michigan while the rest of us made another move.

At 13 years old, I had quickly adopted basketball as my favorite sport, and I didn't like the idea of having to start over again with a new team. Dad saw to it that I played every sport I'd ever wanted to, from hockey to golf. Up until this point, baseball had been my best sport. Even though I was just a big, stubby 13 year-old at the time, I began dreaming about making it big in basketball.

Raising my hand in class to the question of what dreams do you have, I announced to everyone how I was going to play in the NBA when I grew up. The other kids looked at my 200-pound frame and laughed openly. I didn't care. A dream began to be placed in my heart, and I had a God who stood with me and a father who believed I could do anything I wanted. I sat up taller in my homeroom chair.

We had the use of a condo owned by the construction company Dad was working for, which meant we were living in a well-to-do area. Desegregation, however, was taking place with the schools, and a lot of tension existed between the inner-city kids who were being bussed in and the local kids.

Maybe it was because of the tension. Maybe it was because I was the new kid. Maybe it was because he looked like he was 18 and was sore about still being in the eighth grade. Maybe he was just a bully. All I knew was every time I walked down the hallway or had to sit near this kid in class, he smacked me in the back of the head.

I warned him that if he didn't cut it out, I was going to take care of him; he didn't believe me. The next day in science class when he thumped my head again, I surprised myself when I took a chair and hit him in the head with it.

Both of us were forced to go to school on Saturday for eight weeks; nevertheless, I learned something about myself that was an astonishing revelation for me. I could fight back.

Laying in the dark of my bedroom in Michigan, I wondered how it was possible that within a year's time, I had gone from hitting a bully with a chair to fighting grown men on a regular basis. I turned on the light and went to the mirror. "Man, how am I going to explain all these cuts?" I wondered, surprised at how much worse it looked than I thought.

When we came back to Detroit, Michigan, I enrolled in Inter-City Baptist High School and went to live with Mom because Dad was out of work and Mom's situation was financially stable then. Rehabilitation had worked for her; she was totally clean.

My best friend from school, Jason, was especially appreciative of Mom's cooking talents. Every day she made both of us lunches. He readily ditched his own lunch for the one she made us.

Ironically, the very thing that was instrumental in her transformation was also the very thing that caused me the most pain. I had a mom now, but I also had the situations created through the boyfriends she met through rehab. Strong addictive personalities don't belong together.

The police were at our house five and six nights a week because I was constantly fighting boyfriends trying to protect Mom when they knocked her teeth in, bloodied her face and body or broke her leg; fighting seemed to be the one thing I was more talented at than basketball.

Strong and lean, I wasn't made fun of for wanting to be in the NBA anymore. Now they ridiculed me for wearing the same slept-in clothes two days in row, having socks that didn't match or looking like I hadn't slept. What they didn't know was that I didn't sleep a lot of nights because I was up fighting.

I'd seen Mom come home with her bone sticking out her leg. I'd had to follow the instructions of the 911 operator to pull Mom's bottom row of teeth back up so they wouldn't set that way. I'd watched her boyfriend smash her head into the windshield of our little, red Fiero and then follow her into the house punching her in the back of her head as he cussed her out.

I remembered the night my buddy Tom and I came home to find a boyfriend beating on Mom. Mom's boyfriend left with her after I confronted him, but I knew they'd be back. I sent Tom off in the car with Wendy, but I waited on the screened-in porch for them to come back. When they did, I jumped him and beat him so badly he called the police for protection from me, a kid.

The police and I were on a first-name basis. I was standing in the front yard between two policemen while they took his statement in the house. When he came out and began taunting me, it was more than I could handle.

"What are you going to do now, big guy? Not so tough with two policemen around, are you?" He got in my face, "You're the one they are going to be taking away this time, not me."

I saw Mom come to the door, her face swollen and bloody; I knew she wasn't going to press charges. I took my forehead and with all the force in my body, slammed it into his face.

Immediately the police snapped the cuffs on me as they led him away wailing and bleeding. As the officer put me into the car, he reprimanded me in a sympathetic tone, "Chad, you know you can't do that kind of stuff in front of us!"

When Wendy and Tom returned to find me cuffed and in the police car, Wendy became nearly hysterical, thinking I'd killed Mom's boyfriend. I assured her that everything would be fine. The officers somehow convinced the boyfriend not to press charges against me.

All the fighting I did though, didn't prepare me for the day when it was Mom I faced.

CHAPTER 12

AN UNEXPECTED OPPONENT

Mom, when she's clean, is extraordinary; and she was still clean. No drugs, no alcohol. At five foot, nine inches, she is tall, slender, athletic and incredibly beautiful. She knew more about what the latest fashions were than I did. Her thick, blondish-brown hair was always cut in the latest style.

She had been selling cellular phones, and she was good – very good. Once she succeeded in overcoming her addictions, she seemed to succeed at everything she put her mind to, and she wanted me to succeed too.

Mom not only encouraged me in sports, she made sure I had the best opportunities. Aware of the strongest leagues and most competitive schools, she made sure I enrolled in the right ones.

When her boyfriends weren't around, I had a chance to get to know Mom as she genuinely was, without being marred by the effects of alcohol or drugs. That was why what happened next was so damaging to our relationship.

I was coming home from another especially tough basketball practice. The dark sky was dreary as I plodded along Marion Crescent Boulevard; my muscles were sore and aching from the second workout of the day. The house was dark and quiet as I came in and tossed my bag, full of basketball gear on a kitchen chair. "Mom? You home?" I called out. No answer.

I looked in the fridge, but didn't find anything I wanted. I wandered into the living room to watch T.V. That was when I saw Mom. She was sprawled across the couch, clothes a mess. My heart came up in my throat and my voice caught as I choked out, "Aw, Mom. What are you doing? Are you drinking again?"

When I asked those questions, I saw a rage control Mom like I'd never seen before. There were times Mom neglected us because she was passed out. There were times she lashed out at us because she was strung-out; but never had she set out with deliberate attempt to hurt either Wendy or I before. I watched as she transformed into something else, something I had never seen before.

Leaping from the couch, she headed for the kitchen. She was screaming an old familiar tirade at me the whole time, "You don't love me! You never have!" Her voice possessed a tone that caused a chill to run up my spine.

Then I saw what she'd entered the kitchen for – a butcher knife. I ran from her to the other side of the living room and back into the kitchen through its other entrance. She followed me, and we raced in and out of the kitchen several times. On the next pass by the front door, I grabbed the knob with my left hand trying to swing the door open and move through it without letting up speed.

Eyes crazed, Mom thrust the knife toward me and stabbed deep into my arm. When I felt the blade hit bone, everything froze momentarily. I watched blood spatter the stove, cabinets and ugly linoleum floor.

I lunged for the door again and crashed through the screen

door taking it with me down the steps. I threw the door aside and made an open sprint down Marion Crescent. She chased me as I made a right onto West Chicago Street, knife still clenched in her left fist.

Finally, out in the open, I was able to outrun her.

I slowed down and placed my right hand tightly over the gushing wound. I bent down, panting to catch my breath, and tried to think what to do.

Still in disbelief at what had happened, I crossed the street and found a payphone at the Mobil gas station. I dialed the number and sighed with relief when my lifelong best friend, my Cousin Tim, answered on the other end. "Tim, you gotta come get me."

Tim got me to the hospital and fixed up. We went to Dunkin Donuts afterwards and discussed if I should go home or not. "It's O.K. Tim," I told him, "I know the routine. She's long passed out by now."

"What if she comes to?" Tim asked, not convinced it was safe.

"She's gonna be out for hours and hours. Trust me."

"Still, I'd feel better if you came home with me," he said, finishing up his donut.

"You know that won't work," I answered. "You know there isn't room. Your parents have company staying this week; there'd be a lot of embarrassing questions. Please Tim, I don't want the hassle," I begged.

"O.K.," he agreed reluctantly, "but I'm coming home with you."

Glad Tim insisted on staying, I wondered what I would have done without him, as we drove home. It went way past coming to my rescue when I was stabbed and bleeding; his sacrificial acts expressed his unconditional love for me. He was always there for me, so many times he would call me in the mornings to make sure I made it to school, because my life was in so much turmoil I couldn't be counted on to get myself going. I never could quite understand why Tim cared so much for me; all I know is that I could not have made it without him. Tim was more than a best friend; He was like a brother to me.

We crept up to the side of the house where the basement entrance to my bedroom was. Opening the door slowly, we eased into the house. I tiptoed into the living room and looked over on the couch. Sure enough, she was there, totally out.

We headed down the stairs. "Get some sleep," I told Tim as I tossed a sleeping bag his way.

I settled in under my own covers and flipped out the light. Lying on my back, I looked up into the dark. With a deep sigh, I said, "Jesus, give me peace."

Soon, I heard Tim's steady breathing as he fell asleep.

"Jesus does have a purpose for my life," I said out loud in a determined voice, "and, He has a purpose for Mom's life too!" I added defiantly.

Although hurt and confused, I determined I couldn't give up on her any more than Dad had. Hand in a tight fist, I shook my bandaged arm in the air at satan and choked out, "You can't have my mom!"

Hot tears running down my cheeks, through clenched teeth I said, "Jesus does have a purpose for her life. I know it. I saw her come to life after being dead when she overdosed. I was there in Atlanta. I've seen her overcome addiction for years."

I kept praying for Mom, but our relationship changed. I started to focus all my energies into basketball.

CHAPTER 13

PURSUIT
OF A
DREAM

Basketball became my escape from the violent turmoil I was experiencing at home. I averaged well over twenty points a game my sophomore year at Fairlane Christian Academy. Well over six feet tall now, I wasn't called "tubby" anymore. When Mom was clean, she always had my best interests in mind. She saw my potential and knew I needed to be in a high school with a great basketball tradition, if I were going to reach my dream of playing in the NBA. Together we selected Detroit Catholic Central High School.

Not only did Catholic Central afford me exposure on a national level athletically, the academic standards were unsurpassed. Of my graduating class, over ninety percent went to their college of first choice. The more chaos in my home, the more I seemed to excel both athletically and academically.

Coming in as a junior, I was an unknown. This was the seventeenth school I had attended; I moved around too much for any college scouts to possibly recognize me. Even with all the past instability, I averaged twenty-four points a game and twelve rebounds. Finally, college coaches from all over the country began to take notice. My senior year I averaged twenty-eight points, fourteen rebounds and four blocks a game.

Basketball became so much more than an escape from home. It became my life! I began to fulfill the dream of God's purpose for my life through basketball. It was not basketball instead of God; it was basketball with God for me. Before every game, I sat in the locker room writing Scriptures on my game shoes with a permanent marker. Usually, I wrote my favorite verse: Philippians 4:13, "I can do all things through Christ who strengthens me." This was more than just a verse memorized; to me it was a tangible reality.

I played basketball with God at my side. Whenever an interviewer approached me for a line about the game, I gave the glory to Jesus Christ as my living Savior and friend.

Coach Bernie Holowicki put far more than technique into me. He trained me in discipline, determination and dedication. I began to understand the level of discipline necessary to reach my dream of playing in the NBA. I had to give more to basketball than anything else – I had to go beyond even that. I was willing to do whatever it took to make my dreams a reality.

One night we played a game where I scored fifty-seven points. It was the best game of my life; I was hitting three pointers from all over. I had nine dunks. Electrifying excitement and high-fives filled the locker room after the game. My teammates were proud of me.

"Hey, Chad. Great game, man!"

"Chad, come party with us," another offered.

"Naw, I don't think so," I replied, turning back to my locker.

"Why not? You just had the best game of your life. It's time to celebrate!"

"Thanks guys, but I don't think so."

"Come on, Chad," one of the guys coming from the shower

said as he passed my locker, "We aren't asking you to get drunk; man, we know you don't party like that. Just come celebrate with us. You deserve it."

"I have some work to do, guys," I finally said, hoping they would drop the issue.

After my shower, I threw my bag over my shoulder and headed down the hallway. Several children were waiting to get my autograph. Dad was there too. One of the guys saw me and shoved his finger in my ribs as he pushed past, "Chad, you should be partying, man, not going home with your old man. What's wrong with you?"

Finally I reached the car with Dad and shut the door behind all the mocking of my teammates.

"Chad, you just had an incredible game; you should be soaring with enthusiasm. What's wrong?" Dad asked turning the ignition switch.

"Aw, nothing. The guys are just giving me a hard time, you know, 'cause I won't go out and party with them."

"So, what did you tell them?"

"I just told them I had some work to do," I said.

Even Dad looked at me kind of funny, but he dropped it. He knew I didn't party, but he was wondering what kind of work I was intending to do at 11:30 at night in Detroit.

Once home, I put on my shorts and a tank top and went out into the cool night air. I stretched under the dim streetlight, thinking over the game. As I took off for a three-mile run, I told myself, "It's great to be an All-American high school basketball player, but I want more. I want to be the first in my family to graduate from college, and a basketball scholarship is the only possible way. There's no way we can afford the tuition it costs to go to college. Beyond that, my dream is not to score 57 points in a high school baskeball game; my dream is to play in the NBA."

My muscles started to burn as I made the mid-way point and started to head back. Right then and there I decided, "I'm willing to do whatever it takes to get to the NBA." Once I made that kind of commitment, Dad was behind me all the way.

During an important tournament in Ohio I learned the importance of two things. One was a principle Coach Holowicki poured into me, "You don't quit just because you're tired; no matter the circumstances, you keep working as hard as you can." The other thing I learned was the level of Dad's commitment to me and my NBA dream.

CHAPTER 14

A DAD'S SUPPORT

I stepped onto the empty court in Ohio and took a look around before heading to the locker room. I would be playing against 100 of the best high school basketball players in the Midwest for a chance to earn one of 10 spots to the national tournament in Las Vegas.

The morning of the tournament, I played great. When they posted the player cuts, I had made it into the top twenty. In high spirits, I went back to my room to rest before the evening session, knowing if I made the final ten, I would be going to the Las Vegas Invitational. Every college coach in America would be there. Preparing to take an afternoon nap, I took my contact out to clean it, and it tore. I stared down dumbly at the torn contact for a few moments before reacting. "What am I going to do?"

I found a payphone and called home to Michigan. Wendy answered the phone, "Hey, Wen. It's Chad."

"How are you doing?"

"Great, I made it to the final round of try-outs. I tore a contact though."

"Oh, no! You are practically blind without them, how are you going to play?"

"I don't know. Is Dad home?"

"No, he's still working a double at Ford."

"Wendy, I really can't see without the contact. I don't know how I can possibly play like this."

"Well, you'll just have to suck it up and do your best."

"Yeah, you're right," I said with dejection creeping into my voice.

After I hung up, I took a long walk. Knowing I'd have to play with one eye, I focused on doing my very best. I tried not to think about the consequences of blowing this opportunity, and concentrated on doing well. Coach had instilled in me that you have to be committed and persevere regardless of the circumstances. Not playing didn't even cross my mind.

I walked out of the training room after having my ankles taped, prepared for what I thought was going to be the biggest challenge of my life – playing with one eye. No more than ten steps out of the training room, a coach approached, handing me a small box, "Someone just gave this to me to give to you. I think it was your dad. Does he drive a little blue Escort?"

"Yeah," I said uncertainly while opening the box.

I took out the enclosed note as my heart started to race. "Chad, I love you," it read in Dad's familiar writing. "Here's a contact; do your best son, I'm praying for you. I know you can do it!" I let out a whoop, put the contact in and went out to play my hardest.

Afterwards I called Wendy from the same payphone, "Hey, Wen! I got the contact! I'm going to Las Vegas!"

"I called Dad at the plant after I got off the phone with you," Wendy explained. "When he asked about leaving, they gave him a hard time. The only way they agreed to let him go was if he worked another double as soon as he got back. As soon as he gets back from the trip, he's gotta go right back in."

"Where'd he get the money for the contact?"

"I don't know, Chad. He must have borrowed it. He's going to be really glad to hear you made it."

"Tell him he's the best dad in the world and I love him!"

I hung up the phone and pulled the note out of my pocket and read it again. "Thank you Lord!"

I was now a high school All-American. Some recruiting analysts ranked me as high as sixteenth in the nation. To make things even better, I was nominated to the McDonald's All-American team. Soon, I was sorting through scholarship offers from colleges all across the nation.

CHAPTER 15

A FATEFUL PHONE CALL

"What about Florida State University, Chad?" Dad said, handing me their basketball program.

"I don't know Dad," I said, running my hand through my hair, "This is the biggest decision of my basketball life. Everything looks great. It's a great school. I just don't have peace about it."

"Let's go over the information on the University of Richmond again," he said, picking up their promotional packet. I leaned in. "They're not in a major conference, but they have a great team and make the NCAA Tournament just about every year."

"You know what really stands out about it though?" I asked Dad.

"What?"

"Coach Dick Tarrant. He's a proven winner. I know I could start as a freshman, and I would really excel under him. Coach Holowicki always tells me to make sure I pick a school where I can excel."

"It looks to me son like you've made your decision. Why don't you give Coach Tarrant a call and tell him the good news?" Dad said putting an arm around my shoulder.

I entered my first year at Richmond as a highly touted

freshman. Unfortunately, shortly into pre-season conditioning, I developed a season- ending stress fracture in my left foot. I was forced to medical red-shirt, causing me to sit out the entire season. When I learned Coach Tarrant had decided to retire at the end of the season, I began considering my options. The only reason I had decided to play basketball at the University of Richmond was because of Coach Tarrant; thus, I decided to transfer to another university.

I considered another Division 1 university, but since NCAA rules require a player who transfers from one division 1 school to another to sit out one complete year, two years would pass without me having played competitive basketball. That would almost certainly kill my shot at making the NBA. More than anything, I wanted to play.

I weighed several different options. Then I learned that if I transferred to a junior college, I could play the very next season. I quickly researched different schools and found that Vincennes University in Indiana was the top-ranked Juco team in the country. My plan was to play one year at Vincennes, then transfer to another Division 1 school. Besides, Vincennes was ranked number one in the nation, and everybody plays basketball in Indiana.

It was a junior college, however. That posed risks. First, it meant giving up my guaranteed four-year scholarship at Richmond, and Jucos are only two-year schools. If I were injured during the upcoming season, in no way would I obtain another Division 1 scholarship; it would be all over.

After a lot of prayer, I headed to Vincennes for my sophomore year. Once I made the decision, I never looked back, though most people around me thought it was a foolish decision. When I met the most beautiful woman in the world there, Kristie, I knew I'd made one of the best decisions of my life.

Life was awesome. My father continued to support me, basketball was going great and I'd met the love of my life in Kristie. I felt invincible. Then I received the worst phone call of my life. "Chad," Dad said, sounding strained when I answered the phone, "I've got really bad news." Dad took a deep breath, "It's Wendy."

I held the phone with a vise-like grip as I tried to take in the horrific news of a murderous attack against Wendy. She was alive, but she was badly beaten. I made other phone calls, but no one would give me all the details; what I did uncover pierced my heart and I turned my back on the Lord.

Out of fear I would kill the attacker, my father forbade me to leave college. I felt helpless and trapped. I stood in my dorm room and shook my fist at God. "God, you're a phony! You're a joke. I'm not buying into this junk anymore. How could you let this happen to her?" I demanded of God with vengeance. Mom had made her own choices, but Wendy had chosen to live and serve God. I couldn't fathom how He could let harm come to her.

After letting every angry and terrible thing pour out of my heart, I left my room and I forgot about God. I forgot about church. I forgot who I was and whose I was. I turned my back on everything I had ever believed about God and experienced the darkest time of my life. Our whole family ached over what had happened to Wendy, but I was the one who blamed God.

It wasn't until years later that I heard the full story of that horrific Christmas night.

CHAPTER 16

ANOTHER PHONE CALL

Wendy came home from Evangel College where she attended. She was visiting family Christmas night, with a friend of hers named Chris*. They wound up that even going over to Jane's*, a recently divorced relative's house.

Jane had just broken off a tumultuous relationship with her body builder boyfriend named Frank*. Everyone felt uncomfortable when he showed up and it was obvious he'd been drinking. Jane finally convinced him to leave; but his visit left Wendy feeling nervous and uneasy about spending the night with Jane as planned. Chris tried to convince her to come stay with him where he was housesitting.

Wendy knew Chris had honorable intentions, but was concerned about not even entering into the appearance of an inappropriate relationship. Jane was counting on Wendy's spending the night so they could reminisce about old family times and finally coaxed her into staying.

Wendy didn't hear the phone ring at seven o'clock the next morning when Frank called Jane and persuaded her to let him come by to do some laundry. Wendy was still asleep when Jane

*Names have been changed to protect the privacy of the individuals.

followed Frank down the basement stairs to the washing machine. When he sat his basket of clothes down, a crow bar and knife fell out, clanging loudly on the cold cement floor. Instantly, Jane knew he'd come to kill them.

Screaming, Jane raced up the stairs. Awakened by the struggle, Wendy reached the basement doorway to see Frank grab hold of Jane and put her in a head lock, his biceps bulging as he pressed in against Jane's skull. Wendy turned and ran for the back bedroom phone.

Frank followed, dragging Jane like she was a rag doll. Just as Wendy grasped the cordless phone, he reached her and slammed her to the floor. Taking the metal antenna of the phone, he gouged it deep into Jane's face. He pinned Wendy to the floor, then he kicked Jane in the chest and face with the heavy heel of his boot. He began punching both of them in the face with his massive fists in a deranged frenzy.

Without warning, he grabbed both of them by the hair and dragged them back down the basement stairs. Jane's skull hit every step as he made his way closer to the weapons he'd brought. Wendy looked into his crazed eyes, and her heart went cold, as she knew he was about to kill them both. He reached into the basket and pulled out a heavy jute rope.

Wendy had been praying for an opportunity to break his insane furor. As he fumbled with the rope, she announced in a calm voice that she needed to use the bathroom. The controlled tone put him off guard, and he stopped what he was doing. He pushed them both upstairs and let Wendy into the bathroom. As soon as the door was shut, Wendy frantically lunged for the window. She was devastated to find it was a permanent, glass block window. It was impossible to either open or break. Outside the door, Frank had already grown restless waiting. She could hear his fists slamming into Jane's flesh as he let forth a tirade of verbal abuse more filthy than anything she'd ever heard.

Finally he used the force of his massive six-foot–five-inch build to rip the door open. He held the knife to Wendy's throat as he forced them into another room. Bruised and cut, Jane struggled to breathe with broken ribs and teeth knocked in; she could barely move. Wendy's head was split open and both she and Jane were covered in blood. Nevertheless, Wendy remained calm as Frank sat down to smoke some crack cocaine.

"Come on, take some," he demanded.

"No, no," she said convincingly, "You don't want to waste that on me. It's expensive. Save it for yourself." Grateful she was able to protect herself from the drugs, Wendy continued to talk to him as he took his fix and as he came down from it.

Suddenly, Frank snapped into reality. He looked at Jane with her broken nose and bludgeoned face. Wendy was horrified to realize Jane's head had swollen to twice its size. Without warning he began to blubber and cry, sickened at what he'd done.

He went into the hallway and pulled down the attic stairs. When he began making a noose with the rope he'd brought, Wendy realized he intended to hang himself. It was now four hours into their ordeal. She was covered in blood and exhausted from trying to keep one step ahead of him psychologically, but her God was a real God and her relationship with Him more than religious jargon. With the heart of Jesus and genuine concern for his soul, she did the most amazing thing; she talked him out of suicide.

She calmed him by saying things like, "My mom and boyfriends fight all the time, but they always make up. Come on.

Jane will forgive you; you don't have to do this." Finally, Wendy persuaded an exhausted Frank to spare his own life.

Now willing to let them get medical help, he made Wendy first change her and Jane's blood soaked clothes. He carried Jane's limp body to Wendy's car and let them leave before he began his frantic flight from the police.

Barely able to drive, Wendy was shaking and dazed when she spotted a payphone. She screeched to a halt and stumbled to the phone to dial 911. Wendy couldn't wait for the ambulance; she didn't think Jane was going to make it, so she decided to drive to the hospital herself.

Meanwhile, Frank fled across country, beating and holding hostage an elderly couple along the way. He was finally found a month later barricaded in a relative's basement. He is currently in prison serving a long sentence.

Even without knowing these details at the time, I couldn't reconcile Wendy's attack with my knowledge of a loving God. I lived one of the darkest times of my life.

Months later, in the middle of studies one day I got another phone call.

"Hey, Chad." It was Wendy.

"Hey, Wen. How are you doing?" I said in my normal tone of voice.

"What is wrong with you?" Wendy asked, surprised. "You sound so bitter."

"All I said was, 'Hey, Wen,'" I thought to myself. Yet, when she said that to me, a mighty wind of conviction rushed over me. Here she was the one assaulted and traumatized, and she was fine. Suddenly the ugly face of my bitterness confronted me.

"Uh, nothing's wrong Wendy," I managed to choke out. "Look,

I gotta go." I hung up the phone and dropped to my knees in anguish.

"God!" I cried out in desperation, "I am so sorry!"

God had been waiting for me with open arms. As I confessed my bitterness to my heavenly Father, He showed me the selfishness of having picked up the wounds and offenses of others. The strategy satan had used against me became clear, and I felt foolish for having been so easily entrapped by his schemes. Where satan hadn't been able to break me through abuse in my own life, he'd succeeded in getting to me by striking Wendy.

Now, it was like I'd come back to life. With a renewed attitude, I could once again focus on basketball. Kristie and I began to set the foundation of our relationship in Christ. Basketball began to be all I'd ever dreamed it would be. I had a great season at Vincennes – Second-Team, All-American. I was so close to my NBA dream that I could see it. Scholarship offers poured in from all over the nation.

CHAPTER 17

COLLEGE PLAY

"What do we do with all these?" Kristie asked, looking at all the boxes filled with college recruitment offers.

"Well, first we need to narrow our list down to about twelve to fifteen schools. Once we've decided on the schools, the coaches from those universities will come here and try to convince me why I should go to their school. After having those twelve home visits, we then narrow it down to the final five. The NCAA allows five official visits in which the universities will fly me down to their campuses. For three days, they will try to persuade me to come to their school." We sat on the floor evening after evening poring over offers.

One night Kristie said to me, "Some of these are months old Chad, and we haven't even opened them yet; we have do something with all this."

"O.K. Let's see what we've got," I said joining her next to a big box. I reached in and pulled some out. "Hey, what's this?" I said holding up a card envelope.

I opened it up and found it was from Dad. Smiling, I read it. "Look at this," I said handing it to Kristie, "it's postmarked two months ago; it must have gotten mixed in with all this other mail, and I missed it."

Kristie read it aloud, "Dear Chad, I love you, son. I'm proud of you. This is all I could do for you, but I love you and hope it helps."

I looked back in the envelope and found two, one-dollar bills. "Man, this was probably his last two dollars that week," I told Kristie, tears in my eyes.

"Your dad is so incredible!" Kristie said, picking up the bills.

"You know, this means more to me than any of these scholarship offers!"

It took a long time, but after a lot of sorting, sifting and prayer, I finally decided on Kansas, Wake Forest, Wisconsin, Pittsburgh and Missouri.

Coming back to Vincennes after my final visit to the University of Pittsburgh, Kristie asked me, "Well, which one is it?"

"Pittsburgh. No doubt about it," I said. "While I was on my visit, I realized that Coach Ralph Willard has an incredible knowledge of the game, and he likes to play run and gun basketball – that's my style. Our personalities just clicked; I want to play for him. I think he can help get me to the NBA. Plus, they have a great business school."

I learned more about what it took to succeed. Before I left to play my first year in the Big East – the number one conference in the nation at the time – I'd told everybody back home and at Vincennes that I was going to be a starter my first year. I knew I had the skills; after all, I was All-American.

Arriving on campus, I realized that unlike high school ball or playing at the junior college level where I stood out, at Pittsburgh just about everyone on the team was a former high school or Junior

College All-American. Unlike high school ball, where only a few players were willing to go the extra mile in training, I found myself playing with a team full of talented players who were determined to be the best. It took a lot to be willing to do what the other guys wouldn't; college basketball conditioning was already grueling. It was like they had a license to kill us, and we didn't even get paid. Hard work, persistence and diligence became instilled in me.

I found myself competing for a starting position against a veteran team member. We were in the middle of two-a-day practices, practicing mornings and evenings. We were a running, up and down, full-court, pressing team. It didn't take me long to realize the player I was up against had some serious advantages over me. He was older, had more Big East playing experience than me and was physically more developed than I was.

Running sprints and suicides one morning in Fitzgerald Field House, my muscles burning, I wondered if it had been such a wise idea to brag to everyone at home that I'd have a starting position.

Finally, Coach Willard changed his monologue from a relentless, "Don't quit! Run! Suck it up!" to "Alright, hit the showers." Walking off the court, I was looking forward to the hot tub, the training table of food and a chance to rest before the evening practice. Something made me stop dead in my tracks. I remembered how I'd told everyone back home that I was going to start my first year. I realized it would never happen unless I was willing to work harder than the player I was competing against. At that moment, I made a decision. I turned around and headed back to the court.

"Hey," I called out to one of the ball boys, "Would you mind staying an extra twenty or thirty minutes to rebound for me?"

"Sure," he agreed.

From that day on, I believe my understanding about success changed. I stayed after practice day after day working on my jump shot, my crossover dribble and my free throws. I came to a point where I wouldn't leave the court until I made at least ten free throws in a row. My legs burned just as bad as the other guys after practice, but I knew if I wanted to be successful and reach my dream, I had to be willing to do things other guys weren't doing.

When it came time to compete with my teammate for that starting position, I had confidence that I was going to win. Rick Pitino, former head coach of the Boston Celtics and National Champion Kentucky Wildcats, once told me after we spoke at our team's pre-season banquet together that success has to be deserved. You see, I won that starting position because I deserved it. I worked harder than the other guy. I sweated more. I bled more. Success must be deserved! I won the starting position.

My sophomore season, I scored 20 points and grabbed 12 rebounds against the University of Massachusetts, the number one ranked team in the nation. Everything was going great – until I tore ligaments in my hand 10 games into the season. I missed the rest of the regular season. I didn't play again until the Big East Tournament at Madison Square Garden in New York City.

I had an even better junior season, where in Big East play I averaged just over fourteen points and seven rebounds a game. Heading into my senior season I was voted captain. I was also voted a Pre-Season second team All Big East selection, as well as an Honorable Mention All-American by several different media publications. In the summer before my final year at Pittsburgh, I was selected to play on Team America, a collegiate all-star select team. We went over to Italy and played many of the foreign, Olympic teams prior to their coming to play our Dream Team here in Atlanta in the 1996 Olympic games.

Basketball, at this point, was my life, and it afforded me the opportunity to play with some of the best basketball players in the world: Kobe Bryant, Allen Iverson, Tim Duncan, Chris Webber and Ray Allen among others. Coming into my senior season, expectations were high. Everybody in the Pittsburgh, Pennsylvania, area was expecting a great season out of me. Right before the start of the season, however, I developed a stress fracture in my foot. I still played well, but my statistics were affected by the injury.

After college, things were fantastic. I was doing what I loved. Kristie and I had been married now for over two years and were enjoying our first child, Cameron, who was a year old. I was healthier and stronger than I'd ever been and I had financial security; God was blessing me beyond anything the little boy who used to sleep under NBA sheets ever imagined.

"All the turmoil, all the chaos, all the violence is behind me," I told myself just after signing with an agent who was trying to negotiate a deal for me with the Dallas Mavericks of the NBA. "It's all over. Nothing can stop me now. I'm headed for the NBA!"

What happened two days before I was to leave for summer leagues to prepare for training camp changed everything. While I had dealt well with the violence around me, I hadn't even realized the violence that had taken root in me. All I was thinking about was the bright and exciting future before me in the NBA.

CHAPTER 18

BROKEN DREAMS

Getting off the phone with my agent, I headed to the gym in Taylor, Michigan, to work out with a friend. We were in the middle of the workout when Mom came in.

"Chad," she told me earnestly, "I'm finally doing it. I'm not going to be abused anymore. I'm pressing charges, and I need you to come with me to the courthouse for support. Will you do that?"

I hesitated for a moment, "Sure, Mom. Let's go." I left my stuff with my friend and told him I'd be back.

We arrived at the courthouse, and I went in with Mom. As we started to enter the courtroom the clerk stopped us, "I'm sorry sir, you can't go in."

"What? Why?"

"You have to be dressed appropriately for the court, and you are not," he said looking at my tank top and shorts.

I looked down at my sweaty clothes and agreed. "Mom, I'll be right outside. Don't worry, you'll do fine," I tried to encourage her as I turned back to wait. When they brought her boyfriend in, I watched through the window, praying she'd have the strength to go through with her full testimony.

Straining to see through the little window, my heart sank as I realized what was taking place on the other side of the courtroom door. Once again, Mom went soft and told very little of what he'd done. He got off with a restraining order.

"Aw, Mom," I groaned as they came toward the door to leave the courtroom. Her boyfriend swaggered past me to where they had to sign some documents. Standing at the desk, waiting for the lady to get everything in order, he got in my face, "Whaddaya gonna do now, big boy?" he challenged.

I could feel the temperature of my face rising. "Yeah, you're a real man! You can beat up a woman," I shot back.

"You bet I can," he taunted, "and, that's just what I'm going to do as soon as I get her back to the house – beat her face in for getting me put in jail."

He went into a long outburst on Mom, my dad, our family and what he was going to do to Mom when he got her home. All the years of seeing her come through the front door bloodied, with a boyfriend following, bones protruding through her skin, bruises, teeth knocked in, all the years of abuse and violence at the hands of men who thought they were tough by beating on my mom overloaded every circuit in my brain, every thought in my mind and every muscle in my body. I completely lost self-control.

"I'm gonna mess her up bad," he smirked turning back toward the paperwork. With every ounce of power in me, I swung at his head. He turned in just such a way though that my hand caught the back of his head, and I could feel the bones inside snap.

Security was all over both of us within seconds. Before they cuffed me, the lady behind the counter spoke up, "Don't be taking him away! You want to lock somebody up, take him," she said pointing to the boyfriend. "Listen, it wasn't his fault," she told the officers, who believed everything that was said. Miraculously, they let me go. Unfortunately, I was far from being in my right state of mind.

I jumped in the car and raced back to the gym to get my friend and head back. I pulled the car to a stop about 10 blocks from the courthouse. I knew the guy would be walking back to the house instead of riding in the car with Mom due to the restraining order.

As soon as he came around the corner, I jumped him. As I beat him there on the concrete, I thought of all the times I've seen Mom busted and bleeding. I wasn't beating him as much for what he'd done as I was for what I'd seen. Finally, I stopped short and left.

Back in the car, the reality of what I'd done sunk in. It was more than being in trouble with the law for assault now. It was more than having a broken hand. It was more than busting that man up so bad. The reality of the anger I'd let take root in my life scared me.

I dropped off my friend and raced home to Kristie. "We've got to go Kristie. Come on!" I shouted grabbing her.

"Chad, what are you doing?" she asked with a worried look on her face.

"Come on! I'm in trouble – big trouble. We've got to go now!" Confused and frightened, Kristie grabbed our young son, Cameron, and jumped into the car beside me.

"What happened? Where are we going? What did you do to your hand?" she pleaded as we sped down the highway.

"Listen, don't ask me any questions right now; I'm too shook up. We're going to a friend's house. I'll tell you everything when we get there."

Kristie turned and looked out her window. I could tell she was praying. Ten miles later, I took a deep breath and told her everything.

That night as we lay in bed, I repented and then prayed, "God help me. I don't want to react like that ever again." God spoke to me about the violence I'd let take root in myself. I saw clearly the pain it caused the Lord and the damage it did to my spirit. When I confessed to the Lord, a peace came over me and I knew what I had to do.

It was time for me to leave my past behind, time to leave my family and cling to my wife. I decided that day to end taking up the offences of my mom. Realizing she was responsible for the choices she made for her life, not I, I gave it all over to God. Wendy helped me by sending some materials on setting Godly boundaries in my life.

I made two phone calls the next day from my friend's house. One was to find out what charges had been filed against me. "You won't believe this, Chad," Mom told me. "He couldn't press charges!"

"What? You're crazy," I told her.

"No, really Chad. He ran straight back to the courthouse, bleeding and crying. They told him as far as they were concerned he deserved it and to get out. No charges have been filed."

My second phone call was to my agent.

"You did *what*?" he yelled into the phone when I told him I broke my hand (I didn't mention how). "Well, we'll just have to look at some other options."

When I got off the phone, I went to break both the good news and the bad news to Kristie.

CHAPTER 19

CHOICES

I sat next to Kristie on the couch with my hand in a cast. "How is it feeling?" Kristie asked concerned more about my hand than where we were going to go next.

"It's fine," I told her. "Really," I added, giving her a hug.

I sorted through the paperwork strewn across the coffee table. "Kristie," I told her, "with this broken hand, we are left with only two options. Either I go into the CBA (Continental Basketball Association) and work to get fed back into the NBA, or I go play in the European professional leagues."

"Well," Kristie questioned when I hesitated, "what do you think we should do?"

"Look," I said, handing her several sheets of figures, "I've run the numbers over and over; the only sensible thing both for my career and for us financially is to play in Europe. European basketball is so much better now, than it was in the past. The U.S. team barely won the Olympics last time against the Europeans, and our team had all our NBA superstars. Basketball there is good – very good. It will give me the experience I need to get back into the NBA."

"Where?" Kristie asked.

I smiled down at her, "Spain!"

Spain was wonderful. We lived there nine months of the year from 1997 to 1999, traveling nearby when I wasn't playing. We had a beautiful home and vehicles provided as part of my contract. Best of all, we had quality time together as a family. More joy was added to our family when my precious little girl Kiersten was born, while I was playing in Gijon, Spain.

European basketball is very competitive. My skills grew stronger and stronger each year. I was selected to play in the All-Star game each year, including my rookie season.

Going into the second season there, I was playing for Tenerife, Spain, located in the Canary Islands; it is also known as the Hawaii of Europe. We had an incredible team – an incredible year. We were the first place team. I was the team's leading scorer and rebounder, as well as an all-star, for the second consecutive year. My agent was negotiating contracts bigger than I had ever seen. I was invited to play in a prestigious Nike summer league in Travieso, Italy. My future in basketball was finally secured.

God was making sure I knew the significance of family though. I'll never forget the incredible example I had in my father. Dad did much more than just tell us he loved us. He showed us with his actions. We were his priority.

I remember one night in Tenerife. I was sitting on our deck overlooking the Atlantic Ocean, preparing for the evening practice, when I heard Kristie correcting Cameron, our four-year old son. Cameron decided to be an especially defiant preschooler that night. He just refused to do what Mom told him. He was testing us. I took my responsibilities as father of Cameron and Kiersten seriously. I've learned throughout my life that consistency breeds success. Neither Cameron nor I will ever forget what happened that night.

I told Cameron that I was going to sit there and watch him until he did what Mom asked. He continued to refuse. He was determined that his will was stronger than mine. He was wrong.

I finally had to call my coach and tell him I wouldn't be at practice that night because I had to discipline my son. However, one doesn't just miss practice when he's a professional. I was fined a thousand dollars. It was the best thousand I ever spent. I wasn't investing in the stock market; I was investing in my son. People tell Kristie and I all the time how well mannered our children are. There is no secret. Consistency simply works. Your children are a reflection of you; they must be your priority.

As my season in Tenerife was coming to an end, we were anticipating getting back home to the United States. During the three months of the off-season, we lived in Elkhart, Indiana, near Kristie's family. That was part of the deal. Kristie told me before we ever left for Spain that if I was going to take her across the world, during the off-season we had to live by her family. I did what all good husbands do – I agreed!

I'll never forget the night I had one of my best games of my professional career. I scored 36 points and pulled down 19 rebounds. We were in first place. After the game, Kristie, the kids and I went to a restaurant to celebrate, with some of the other married couples from my team. Kristie left early with the children so they could get a good night's sleep.

A short time later, I came home exhilarated, knowing the game would be all over television and the newspapers the next morning. I checked in on, and prayed over Cameron and Kiersten and climbed in bed, giving Kristie, who was already asleep, a kiss before falling asleep myself.

Two-thirty in the morning, I was startled wide-awake. I couldn't sleep. I rubbed my face and wondered what was going on. I knew I was exhausted because I had just played a forty-minute game. Feeling the prompting of the Holy Spirit, I threw back the sheets and went into the kitchen. I laid my Bible out before me, and God took me from Scripture to Scripture. I wrote Scriptures on several pieces of paper and then taped them all over the house. I wept that night like a baby, knowing that God was birthing something inside of me.

In the midst of being happier and more successful in basketball than I'd ever been, I began to realize life could offer more than dunking a basketball. God was gently showing me that when Wendy knelt and prayed that prayer for us about God having a purpose for our lives, He meant more than professional and material success.

I wasn't sure what God had in mind, but by the time I headed back to bed, the call of God upon my life was being branded on my heart. Treasuring that night, I finished out the season and signed with one of the top agents in the world.

Professionally, teams from all over the world were interested in me. My future was looking incredible. I had several six-figure contracts, on the table for the upcoming season. We'd been doing well financially, but because of the season I just finished, I knew the next year was going to be even better. Having earned my bachelor's degree from the University of Pittsburgh, I had been careful to make wise financial decisions. While in Europe, we were provided with everything needed - the house, the vehicles, they even paid our taxes. When we came home to the states for three months, we were careful not to overspend and we paid off debt. Since we were out of the country for nine months each year, we secured short-term leases on a vehicle and furnished suite when we were back home in Elkhart, Indiana.

Because we knew a big contract was coming, we incurred some short-term debt. We planned to eliminate that with the first check of the up-coming season. Then, we would be debt free and in a position to buy a house, build some equity and get that red, Lincoln Navigator I'd been thinking about. I wanted to get Dad a house as well.

My agent was sifting through the offers, giving me the best ones to review. The main contract we were considering was sixty-thousand dollars the first month, thirty-thousand dollars a month after that, and laced with incentives – a thousand dollar bonus for every game I scored more than twenty points, a thousand dollar bonus for every game I had over ten rebounds. As we packed up and headed home for our annual three-month break in Indiana though, it wasn't the decision of which team I'd choose that puzzled me. Instead, as my family and I flew across the Atlantic, I wrestled with if I'd ever play basketball again.

CHAPTER 20

STRUGGLING WITH THE CALL

I looked over at Kristie in the airplane seat next to me. "I've always relied on the Lord whenever I've made decisions," I told her, "but this is different. We're going to need numerous solid confirmations before we can even think about giving up basketball."

Ministers usually say you need two or three confirmations before you go into the ministry. God didn't disappoint us. Confirmation after confirmation of a call on my life to head into ministry flooded over me during our time in Elkhart, Indiana. I couldn't ignore the certainty of it.

Finally, I stopped asking myself "if" questions and focused on the "when" questions. "When does God want me to do this?" I asked myself over and over. "Certainly, it makes sense to play another season or so, get financially prepared, then step out." I was talking to myself a lot those days.

Throughout our struggles with this new call, our pastor, Paul Furrow at Calvary Assembly of God in Elkhart, provided tremendous support. He went beyond just giving me ministry advice. He instructed me in how to know the will of God for my life. Sitting down with me, he listed the pros and cons of the two options I was examining.

I contemplated playing for another year or two, pursuing ministry training, preparing the ground, gathering advice, setting up a financial ministry base and then when everything was stable, fulfilling the call.

I also weighed the option of stepping straight out into the unknown.

In the midst of decision-making, I went into the gym at Calvary Assembly of God. I spun my ball out in front of me and started shooting jump shots. With every ball that swished through the net, I thought of another thing that giving up basketball right then would mean. I thought of how we lived right on the Atlantic Ocean in Tenerife. I thought of the swimming pools, the tennis courts and the new full size Mitsubishi Montero sport utility vehicle the team provided while I was in Spain. I thought of the miniature golf course I took the children to on the seventh floor of our complex. I thought of the future financial security for our family, for our children.

I was twenty-five with no broken bones; I was in the best shape of my life and at the peak of my career. I wasn't at a point where I needed to retire. I'd just signed with one of the top agents in the world. I liked the feel of the energy flowing through my muscles as I dribbled up and down the court of the church gym, knowing I was playing at the best level I'd ever played, an NBA playing level. I thought of playing before live crowds of tens of thousands of people and playing on television before millions.

I started shooting free throws, trying to make twenty-five in a row as I asked myself if I could give up basketball. I thought back to college and then high school, remembering the sacrifices success demanded. Success comes with a price. I remembered cutting the cast off my broken hand, just two weeks into the six-week healing period so I could force my hand into playing condition to be ready to try out for Gijon Baloncesto, my first team in Europe.

I knew it was going to take the same level of commitment to be willing to do what others aren't in ministry if I were going to make it. Already people in ministry whom I respected had discouraged me by telling me I'd just be a testimony guy; there wouldn't be any substance in my ministry to preach the Word with authority. They pointed out my total absence of training. After all, I hadn't gone to Bible College.

I started running suicides hard up and down the court as I thought of a generation of young people who had never been exposed to Jesus. Someone has to bring hope to the kids who see their moms beaten night after night like I did, to the ones who are being beaten and abused in ways that are unimaginable to me, even in the violent environment in which I grew-up. I thought of what basketball had given me in escaping the living hell of my childhood, and I wondered if I could let it go.

Suddenly I realized that if I gave up basketball, it would take away something I'd relied on nearly my whole life for escape, hope and a future. If I gave up basketball, I'd be stripped of everything I'd ever depended on – except my relationship with Jesus. With this realization, I dropped to my knees, sweat pouring off my body and cried out to God in anguish as the very real existence of the spiritual battle I was facing pressed in on me.

Getting off the floor, I found it was much later than I realized. There was a service that night I didn't want to miss. I rushed out of the gym to make it home in time to get ready.

CHAPTER 21

INSPIRATIONAL LAUGHTER

Convinced of the call, but struggling with the particulars, I loaded up the family to hear an evangelist who had come in to preach at our church in Elkhart. I wasn't familiar with him, and he had no idea who I was; I was just another member of the congregation that night.

After preaching a powerful message, the evangelist crossed the platform and stopped right in front of me. He reached out and pointed straight at me in the fourth row. "What's your name?" he asked.

"My name is Chad," I answered.

"Son, the Holy Spirit just told me you're wrestling with the call of God on your life," he said, giving me a clear and steady gaze, "and, God is telling you to step!"

As the words reached my ears, my spirit surrendered totally. I knew it was over. The struggling with the decision, the uncertainty about the call and the questions about timing – they were all over. More significantly, I knew basketball was over.

Early the next morning, I phoned my agent and told him I was turning down the contracts and money because God had a call on my life. He couldn't even begin to understand the decision we'd made. He probably thought I was just another athlete who had a so-called "experience with God."

God reinforced in us the importance of stepping out in His timing with an all too real illustration. One of the contract offers we had considered was in Istanbul, Turkey. We knew the basketball there was great and the money was excellent. Neither Kristie nor I had a peace in our spirits over it and had turned it down.

If we had taken that contract, we would have already been in Turkey. Shortly after we made our decision not to accept the contract, an enormous earthquake hit just outside the capital city Istanbul, killing 17,000 people. "Would we or our children have been killed too?" Kristie and I asked each other. We didn't know, but we felt God was imparting into us the need to step out in faith. When he told us to, never too soon and never too late. It helped give us the confidence to move forward here.

"What now?" I wondered. Basketball was my only source of income. My first two years playing professionally, we made great money. I was disciplined financially, and we paid off debt. I always set aside plenty of finances to live comfortably for the three months we were home. My plans had been that after my first two years of paying off debt, I would sign a big contract. We would be debt free and able to do the things we'd always dreamed of doing. Suddenly though, we had no security; the finances I had set aside quickly dwindled as our time home rapidly approached four-and-a-half months. The reality of our financial situation was heavy.

I'd walked away from the only career I had known. We had nothing – no car, no home. We'd returned the leased car already and the rent was due on our furnished suite in just eight days. The forty thousand dollars worth of debt we still had suddenly seemed huge. When I knew I'd be signing that contract at sixty thousand dollars for the first month - it seemed a minor hindrance, I'd write the check for $40,000 and put the rest in the bank. No big deal. Suddenly, that debt felt like a lifelong bondage. I had just made the biggest – without a doubt the craziest – decision of my life: I'd chosen to leave basketball and establish myself in ministry – a ministry with no bookings. I had never preached. I didn't have any promotional material to send to pastors. I'd made the transition, but I didn't know how I was going to take care of my family.

I spent a late night counseling with our pastoral staff, sorting through not just the spiritual issues, but also the very real issues of how I was going to properly provide for my family.

In the morning, I arose early to have devotions with the Lord as usual when satan began to try to discourage and humiliate me. "Chad, listen," I could hear him saying, "you need to go back. You need to play. You know, at least one more year.

"How you gonna make it? Huh? You're supposed to be the man of the house, the provider; you can't even pay the rent without basketball.

"Who do you think you are? You don't know the first thing about ministry. What pastor is gonna want to have you come speak? Be serious. You can't even send them a tape of yourself preaching to consider because you've never preached. Are you nuts? You better call your agent back and tell him you're going to play next year; just give it up."

The more I wrestled spiritually, the more frustration emerged. Going out into the living room, feeling agitated, I called Kristie and the kids into the living room. I told them to get in a circle and hold hands. I grabbed five-year-old Cameron and Kristie held onto two-year-old Kiersten.

Kristie hadn't questioned me aloud once. Yet, I wondered if she was going to be able to have the faith to stand by me through all this. "I am supposed to be the provider," I said sarcastically to myself. I knew that Kristie had grown up in a good home, but not one where she had seen the miracles of faith I'd seen. "What kind of strain is this going to put on us?" I questioned.

Suddenly, it hit me.

I turned to Kristie and said firmly, "Laugh!"

She looked back at me like I was a lunatic and gave out a fake, "Ha. Ha. Ha."

I leaned in close and said with the same fake tone, "Ha. Ha. Ha."

Cameron and Kiersten didn't get it, but they certainly thought Mom and Dad looked like the two biggest clowns they'd ever seen. They began to giggle with genuine laughter.

Kristie and I looked down at them. She looked back to me and we both burst out laughing. Soon, none of us could stop, even though we wanted to. I tumbled onto the floor and took Cameron down with me. Kiersten rolled on the floor squealing with delight. Soon Kristie was on the floor too.

All the tension melted. All the agitation lifted. All the pressure disappeared. This story may sound crazy, but as I lay there on the floor, I remembered one of the principles from the Scriptures the Lord and I went over together that night in Tenerife when He revealed my call. "I will have joy in the midst of adversity and God will carry us through."

I could have walked out into that living room and said, "What are we going to do? Our rent is due in eight days." Or, Kristie could have challenged me to do something because our situation proved financially impossible. A heated argument could have arisen. Instead, we chose to have joy in a time of adversity. We were still piled up on the floor, wiping the tears of laughter from our eyes, when the phone rang.

CHAPTER 22

NEW HOME PROVIDED

"Chad," Pastor Furrow was saying on the other end of the line, "I know the decision you've made is from God; I think we have the solution to your rent problem."

"Great!" I responded, thinking God had come through with the money to pay the rent of our furnished suite.

"Last night I talked to one of the ladies in our congregation. She says it's her heart to open up their house for people. She feels like that is their calling, their ministry," Pastor Furrow explained, obviously excited about how quickly the Lord was moving to provide for us.

Hundreds of thoughts were running through my mind all at once. "Us, live with someone else? I don't know. What about Kristie? We've lived very comfortably these past couple of years, how is she going to give this all up at once? What about sharing a house with virtual strangers?"

I realized that stepping out into the ministry in the way God had called us to meant great sacrifice. I suspected He was trying to strip us of any possessiveness over material possessions. I also suspected He was working on my pride, and that He intended to prove Himself as our provider.

After a much too long pause, I replied, "That's great, Pastor. Who is it?"

"It's Beverly and Gordon Foster," he answered.

"I'll tell you what," Pastor Furrow continued, "I'll have Pastor Jim Williams, the business administrator of the church, take you over and you can discuss the arrangements with Beverly and Gordon."

"Sure," I said a little too weakly.

Jim picked me up, and we headed over. On the way, he put in a call to the Fosters. Gordon answered the phone, and it was all too obvious from his confusion that he had no idea what Beverly had offered. I began to feel a little weaker.

Beverly greeted us warmly at the door and led us into the living room where Gordon was waiting. I could sense the tension in the room.

Beverly filled Gordon in on the offer she had made, and I began to share what our needs were and what God was doing in our lives. The Spirit of God fell, and a heavy presence of the Lord filled the room. Tears began to well up in Gordon's eyes. He told us that he felt good about the arrangement, and we settled all the details to move in within the week.

Now I just had to go home and explain it all to Kristie. When I went home, I was nervous because I didn't know how Kristie would respond. We'd both become accustomed to the lifestyle we'd been living. Now I would be asking her to give it all up and move in with people we didn't even know.

When I explained the offer to her, I realized just what I had in Kristie. She looked me in the eyes and told me if this was part of the road we had to follow to get to the vision God gave me, then she refused to question the situation. "This is a God thing, Chad," she said firmly, "Let's do it."

Several days later, I collapsed onto the sofa in the living room, "Phew, that's the last box."

"Here, have a caffeine-free Diet Pepsi," Gordon offered, sitting in the chair opposite to me.

We began to discuss the move, the house and the church. I discovered Gordon had been estranged from the church for over 20 years. I began to share in earnest how I had seen God work in my life over and over again and the spiritual principles God had imparted to me.

"Well," I finally said, "I suppose Kristie and the kids are already asleep. I better let you get some rest too. Thanks again for your hospitality."

"Goodnight," Gordon said, picking up the pop cans and taking them into the kitchen.

The first Sunday in the Foster home, we all headed out for church. Pastor Furrow gave an anointed message as usual. A man with a heart for souls, he drew people to the altar. I have never been in one of his services where at least one person didn't get saved. During the altar call, I noticed a figure to my left practically bolt to the altar. I did a double take; it was Gordon Foster!

Both Pastor Jim and I jumped into the air with joy, hands lifted high. We raced down to the altar to be with him. Gordon rededicated his life to the Lord, and the beginning of a deep and meaningful relationship was formed.

Within days, Kristie and I felt the depth of the relationship that would be formed with Beverly and Gordon; they were becoming like a second mother and father for both of us. Our children loved them. We were so grateful to the Lord for giving us the honor of being placed in their home; we realized how far beyond our own means the provision of the Lord goes.

Now I just needed to find some place to minister.

CHAPTER 23

STEPPING OUT!

Now settled into the house, early the next morning I phoned Pastor Furrow. "Listen, Pastor," I said, "would it be alright if I use the boardroom upstairs in the church to make some phone calls?"

"Sure," he replied a little uncertainly. "What for?"

"I have to start scheduling speaking dates," I reported confidently, unaware of how difficult it would prove to be.

Arriving at the church, I peeked my head around the corner of Pastor's office on my way up to the boardroom. "By the way," I asked, "do you have one of those church directory books with all the church addresses and phone numbers?" Pastor Furrow smiled and tossed me a little red book.

I was determined to step out into the new call immediately. A great friend and mentor, Tony Brock, had once said to me that two-thirds of the word "God" is "go." I intended to go forward, full-speed ahead.

It wasn't long before the reality of the challenges began to sink in. I was virtually unknown. I had no pastoral contacts. Secretaries wanted to know my qualifications and experience. I didn't have any experience. Assistants wanted me to send audiotapes and videotapes of my speaking. I didn't have any tapes. They suggested I send one of my ministry brochures. I didn't have any brochures.

I continued to call churches at random. I restricted myself to Indiana, where I was currently living, the Pittsburgh area, because that was where I played college ball, and Michigan and Ohio, because I lived there growing up. Rejections came, but God's favor was upon me as well.

"Listen, let me tell you what is going on in my life," I would tell any pastor who would listen. "Just three days ago, I gave up a lucrative career in professional basketball. God has put a passion in my heart to reach the lost. God has done some incredible things in my life. Can you give me just ten minutes to share a little of it with you?"

Pastors and secretaries began to listen to me pour out my heart. Soon I was scheduling dates. I had no idea if the churches were big, small, urban, multi-media or what. I just knew I had to tell people what God had done in my life – anywhere He would allow me.

Without any promotional material, no tri-fold brochures and not a single audiocassette, I booked three months solid in just three days. I was astounded at the confirmation of God's call.

A really surprising thing happened next; I received a call from a church. They must have heard about me from my pastor, I reasoned. The lady told me they were opening a youth facility and they wanted me to be their grand-opening speaker.

I got off the phone and gave Kristie a high-five. "They want me to be their *grand-opening* speaker!"

A few days later, I was headed for the event in our conversion van. A typical lake-effect snowstorm was underway. I struggled through the snow to make it to Granger, Indiana. "It's worth it though," I told myself, wondering how big of a facility it was going to be.

I pulled into the parking lot and I looked back at my directions. "This can't be it." I said confused. The pastor immediately met me and didn't even take me toward the church – we headed for the parsonage.

About three-fourths of the way down the basement stairs, I looked over and saw a little convenience store type machine twirling hot dogs. A few bags of open chips lay next to some pop cans on a folding table.

Looking past the snack table, I saw the chairs set up for the evening – twelve of them. Four kids were sitting together talking on the front row. I stopped dead in my tracks and said to the Lord, "God, you called me away from basketball for this? I've played in front of millions of people on TV. I've been on the cover of several different magazines. You told me to leave basketball to speak to four kids?"

God's rebuke was like a strong upper cut to my jaw. I flinched with conviction when He answered me, "Chad, I didn't call you to be successful; I called you to be obedient."

By the time my foot hit the next step my attitude was straightened out. I gave my testimony to those four kids with every ounce of passion the Lord had given me.

As one of the kids came forward to receive the Lord as his Savior, I knew it wasn't about hundreds or thousands; it was about each individual. It was about being obedient to the call of God on my life, no matter what capacity He chose for me.

Once again, God drove home the point with me that He was doing a quick work with my call. He had addressed the issue of pride in my life that night by not letting me get caught up with self-importance. He'd also worked hard on my pride concerning my ability to provide for our family versus just trusting Him for provision.

I had a lot of trouble accepting the honorariums the churches presented. I had trouble receiving. Churches would offer me an honorarium when I was finished sharing my testimony, but I couldn't receive. I would sign checks back over to the churches or give them to other ministries. God had to work hard to break the issues of pride in my life so He could use me.

After my first week of traveling, I realized I had much to learn about being more effective. Although I had a passion to challenge the churches, I also had a burning passion deep inside me to reach a generation of kids searching for something real, searching for a God who cares about them personally.

I decided I needed to contact the best of the best at reaching kids in the public schools. I only considered one man.

CHAPTER 24

AN OPPORTUNITY OF A LIFETIME

"What?" Tim practically yelled into the phone from his office in Griffin, Georgia, where he was now a youth pastor. "What are you talking about, Chad?"

"Listen," I said into the phone to my cousin and best friend, Tim Bach, "Just give me the number."

"Look Chad, I know we've talked all this over already, but are you sure you know what you're doing? Do you have any idea what kind of capital you need to run a ministry like you're talking about?" Tim was trying to reason with me.

"Tim," I said patiently, "just give me the phone number."

"Chad, an evangelist is here with me at the church; you know him. Let me talk all this over with him and see what he thinks about this whole decision you've made. I'll call you right back."

"Fine," I sighed into the phone.

Only a short time passed before the phone rang again. "Well?" I said to Tim.

"Listen Chad, we've talked it over, and it just doesn't seem to make sense, you know. I mean, you've got it made. Play basketball for at least another year. You don't have to step out right away.

Get yourself some training first. You need to learn homiletics and exegesis. Besides, without finances, it's going to be so hard for you to make it."

"Tim, I know it's important to get training before I go into the ministry. That's what I'm trying to do here. Give me the phone number! Besides, you know this is different, Tim. God hasn't called me to do this in the future; He's called me to do it now." I sighed again, "Look, I know you're behind me, man. I have to be obedient to both the call and the timing," I explained. "Now, please give me his phone number."

"Sure, Chad," Tim said adding, "but you'll never get through to him yourself."

"Just give me the number and let me worry about that."

Dave Roever's number in hand, I sat down to make the call.

Eight months into his duty in Vietnam, Dave was burned beyond recognition when a phosphorous grenade he was poised to throw exploded in his hand. Both his survival and life are testimonies of the miraculous hand of God.

Using his war experiences of loneliness, peer pressure, disfigurement and pain as well as a life of integrity through his relationships to his parents, wife and children, Dave reaches youth with a message of hope. Since 1976, Dave has spoken face-to-face with almost six million students in the public schools. I knew Dave Roever could help me.

Even after scheduling three months of speaking, I was unprepared for the size of ministry I was calling. Somehow I convinced the last person in a long chain to switch me through to Dave's scheduling director, Louise.

"Hello, is Dave Roever there?" I asked for what seemed like the tenth time.

"No . . .," Louise said, "Honey, who is this?"

"This is Chad Varga," I replied, "My cousin Tim Bach used to travel with Dave. Do you remember him?"

"Oh, yes! I know Tim; we love him," she said warming up.

"Well, let me tell you about how I've just left basketball," I began, condensing most of my testimony into the shortest possible time ever. "I just need to pick Dave's brain. I feel God calling me to the public schools, and I know Dave is the best of the best at that. God has used him so mightily, and I need some guidance. If I could just talk to him for a short while."

"Honey," Louise said sympathetically, "I'm sorry to tell you, he's leaving in a few days and will be gone for three weeks. It's going to be quite a while before he can get back to you."

"Can I leave a message on his voice mail then?" I asked, thinking quickly.

"Honey," she said, "you're talking to his voice mail."

"Well, when can he get back to me?" I asked hopefully.

"Look, it'll be three weeks before even I talk to him. At least a month before he gets back to you," I heard a click, and before I could answer, she said, "Hold please," and was gone.

After five minutes on hold, I started pacing the floor. "Man, this is long distance," I said to myself, "I'm going to have to pay Beverly and Gordon for this; I wish she'd hurry up!"

Finally, Louise came back on the line, "Chad? Is that right?"

"Yes."

"You're not going to believe this, honey, but Dave just called, and he's on the other line. He wants to take your call."

Fireworks went off in my spirit. I breathed a prayer of extravagant gratitude the Lord's way. Graciously, Dave allowed me to share for 15 minutes my testimony, call and passion.

The Holy Spirit came over Dave, and he told me the confirmation he felt in his spirit. He wanted me to do schools with him. "I'll fly you down to Fort Worth and we can talk about it," Dave told me.

In Fort Worth, I spent the day with Dave and his wife Brenda. Dave had mentored and poured his life into so many great ministers over the years that I was more than honored when he said he was willing to let me travel with him for three months.

"There's just one problem, Chad," Dave said, "I'm struggling with a lower back problem. After this trip, I'm taking a rest for a few months. I'd like you to travel with me after that."

I didn't hesitate. We got Louise on the line and did all the necessary scheduling. I marveled at the Lord's timing; my time with Dave started the Sunday after the three months of engagements I had already booked myself. I was overwhelmed at the favor of God on this ministry. I don't call it my ministry, because it's not; it's the ministry God called me to, and I can see that when He is in total control, His favor is there.

God worked more on my pride during the remainder of the three months when I went out on my own, especially in a little place called East Tawas, Michigan.

CHAPTER 25

"WHAT'S YOUR DEBT?"

I pulled into the church at East Tawas, Michigan – population 2,887. It was the fifth place I was scheduled to speak. Homiletically structured, or not, God had given me a word to preach beyond sharing my testimony, and I was determined to share it with these people.

Beginning to feel like a proper evangelist, I gave an altar call following my message and began to pray for those of the congregation who had come forward. I looked up after praying for one woman and noticed a man waiting for me in ripped blue jeans and a plaid, flannel shirt. "Naturally, this man has come up to get his life right with the Lord," I thought to myself, ready to pray my heart out. Aloud, I asked, "You want me to pray for you?"

"No, Brother Varga," he said, "I have a question for you: what's your debt?"

I tried to not to betray how taken aback I was. I replied respectfully, "Sir, I'm doing fine," and started to turn away.

"I asked you, what's your debt?"

Frustrated, I looked at his red flannel shirt, to his jeans, on down to his tan work boots, "Sir, God's providing. We're doing fine."

I couldn't believe this guy would ask me something so personal. Nobody knew my financial situation. I didn't know it, but I was struggling with pride.

"Brother Chad," the gentleman said more firmly, "I was sitting in the second to the last row during service, and the Holy Spirit told me to come up here and ask you, 'What's your debt?' Now then, what's your debt?"

Not wanting to be an offense for the Holy Spirit, I gave a straightforward reply, "About forty grand."

"Well, then," he said, as if the matter was settled, "we're going to take care of that for you."

I thought to myself, "That's sweet. I appreciate his faith. What's he gonna do? Mail it to me?" Even in my short time in ministry, I had heard that one before. I didn't expect anything as I went back to wrapping up the service.

Cameron, who was traveling with me while Kristie and Kiersten were at home participating in a women's meeting, climbed into the van ahead of me. As we watched the snow falling, we waited to follow the pastor to lunch. I noticed instead, in my side mirror, Pastor Quinn Mckenzie trudging through the snow up to the van window. I rolled down the window. He looked me in the eye and said a phrase I will never forget. "Chad," he said, "I'm a simple man. I live a simple life. But, we don't serve a simple God." Then he handed me a $40,000 check from Jim Fairbanks, president of Rising Eagle Enterprise, the developer of the process for recycling disposable camera cases for multi-use – the man in the flannel and torn blue jeans.

Even though the wind and snow were stinging my face with cold, I felt my face flush as I said, "Sir, I can't take this."

I hesitated, remembering what the Lord had already been teaching me about receiving. I'd been telling Kristie for weeks, "You'll see, Kristie. Someone might just walk up to us and hand us a check for forty grand. It could happen."

He looked surprised as I handed it back and explained, "I'll tell you what, I'll send you all the names and addresses of where we owe the debt, and you send it directly to them. That way, both you and I know that every penny will go where it rightly belongs."

God was doing a dual work. He was adjusting my pride and showing me how not to make on-the-spot judgments of people. He was also building my wife's faith. Kristie hadn't grown up seeing miracles in her life; she didn't grow up in church. When we left basketball, one of her biggest concerns was how we were going to pay off that forty grand. Providing like He did was God's way of showing her that she didn't need Chad's basketball to take care of her. God had given us a promise when we left the basketball world: "I'll never leave you nor forsake you."

As I continued to travel and preach in churches, God blessed my obedience. I preached in churches of fifteen people and churches of three thousand. God opened the doors for me; it was all him, not my abilities. I had no promotional material, no big name.

I loved my time with people who loved God and wanted to serve Him, but the passion in my heart for young people was growing and burning red-hot. I was anxious to begin going out to where the hurting kids were. I was yearning for my time with Dave Roever.

CHAPTER 26

TIME WITH THE BEST

I soon discovered that not only was Dave the best of the best in doing public school assemblies, but he was outstanding as a mentor. He trained me in authority, leadership, humility, and the importance of being ready in season and out as well as in a multitude of practical areas. God demonstrated powerfully through my time with Dave not just how to be blessed and receive, but how to be a blessing.

Up until this point, my family had traveled with me 99% of the time; I don't believe God has called me into the ministry to neglect my family. So, when the first trip with Dave was a ten-day stint, I reeled a little at the thought of being away from them that long.

As I watched Dave though, it was all worth it. He is a master communicator, and I became a sponge soaking up every bit of knowledge, every bit of insight and every facet of how to deal with school administrators in a respectful and Godly manner. I learned about Dave's heart and passion for a lost and hurting generation. Most importantly, I noticed that Dave is about more than his own ministry. He is a reproducer. He doesn't just impact audiences, he influences other ministers who go out and affect other audiences. He will have a legacy that goes far beyond his own ministry because of the way he has not just added to the kingdom, but multiplied through like ministers.

Through his own passion for the continuation of ministry, he coached me in the difference between reward and credit. He asked me one day, "Chad, do you want the credit or the reward? You see, getting the credit means earthly praise and recognition for what you do in life, in ministry. Getting the reward though! That's God's praise, and it doesn't even compare to the other. Never worry about who gets the credit; always seek the reward."

More than anything else though, his confidence in my call and ministry impacted me. Actively demonstrating his belief in my call, he gave me as much as thirty minutes of a forty-five minute assembly at times, allowing me to pour into the kids with all my heart.

Two incredible miracles took place during my first trip out with Dave that grounded me in an important Biblical principle concerning financial blessings. Right before we left, a medical situation came up with my father that required $1,300. Once again, I told Kristie that I knew God would come through. Nevertheless, it was on my mind during the trip.

We were on the last leg of the journey, riding in the tour bus, when Dave turned to me, "Now, Chad," he told me seriously, "I better tell you a little about this next church we are going to. They're good people, but," he leaned a little closer, "they're just a little different crowd. You've already seen in the schools where there is a difference in crowds. Some follow you easily; others are more... difficult. Well, this church is more on the side of difficult. They are just, you know, not very responsive."

Surprised, I determined to watch Dave even more closely while he spoke to learn how to handle an apathetic audience. We walked up on the platform during worship, and I was a little astounded; it was enthusiastic and powerful. "What's Dave talking about, unresponsive?" I wondered. Still, my eyes and ears were going to be glued to Dave the whole time.

The order of service came to the time for Dave to speak. Just before he rose to get up, he leaned over to me and whispered, "By the way, Chad, you have the service tonight." Then he walked up to the podium and took five or ten minutes to talk about his ministry and introduce me while I was wondering how I was going to approach what Dave had led me to believe was going to be very difficult.

Dave smiled broadly as I rose to speak. I was prepared though, and I spoke with passion. Just a few minutes into my time, I realized Dave had just been teasing me about the congregation; they were great and went well beyond "responsive."

God moved at the altar time, and I left the church feeling incredibly blessed. I arrived at the tour bus. Kristie called me on the cell phone, and I excitedly told her how the Lord had moved. Then she asked, "Chad, what are we going to do about the $1,300 for your dad? We still don't have it."

"Well, Kristie," I told her, "We have to do it. Go ahead and put it on the credit card in the morning; we'll just have to make it work."

Kristie agreed, and I walked into the bus. Dave and I chatted for a while, and he said, "Chad, great job tonight. You were ready in season and out. That's what I wanted to see; could you be prayed-up and ready to represent God on a moment's notice if you had to." I was grateful for his words of confidence. "I want to tell you what the church did though," he continued. "They were really moved by what took place tonight; they wanted to bless you financially."

"Alright."

Dave handed me a check, and I looked down at it. It was written for $1,350! Once again, God taught me about his provision.

The next morning the pastor of the church gave me a ride to Mobile, Alabama, to catch my flight back home. God wasn't through with my lesson concerning the receiving of the $1,350; He had more to tell me in the airport.

CHAPTER 27

AIRPORT BLESSINGS

Locking my seatbelt in place, I leaned back in my airplane seat, glad to be on my way home. Before long, the flight attendant came over the speaker. Instead of the usually emergency instructions though, she said, "We are sorry to inform you that we are experiencing mechanical problems. We must ask that you all de-board."

Frustrated by the four-hour delay, I plopped down on a hard plastic seat in the airport. I considered calling Kristie to let her know I'd be late, but realized it was too early in the morning.

Finally, I rested my head in my open hands to spend some time talking to God about how thankful I was for the opportunities He was providing me with Dave Roever, for the way He had moved the night before and for the financial blessing of $1,350.

Suddenly I felt the Holy Spirit speak to me, and I looked up. Across the way at the airline counter I noticed a couple obviously having some difficulty with the agent. I put my head back down and felt the Holy Spirit say, "Chad, you need to bless that couple financially."

Having trouble receiving blessings, I reasoned that I must have been trying to justify receiving the $1,350. Then the thought came stronger to bless the couple.

Just as I looked up again, they were about to pass by me with their luggage. I said, "Sir, what was the problem at the counter?"

With a heavy African accent he answered, "They say our bags are too heavy."

"Oh," I said understanding about extra charges for going over weight limits. "How much do they want to charge you?"

"One hundred and forty dollars. Seventy dollars for each of these two bags," he said indicating the suitcases.

I stood and put my arm on his shoulder, "Sir, do you know Jesus Christ?"

"Yes, Sir!"

"Well, Sir, Jesus has blessed me more in my life than I can even begin to explain. I don't have any idea who you are, but the Holy Spirit told me that you don't need to carry this financial burden."

I pulled out my wallet and took out seven of the fifteen twenty dollar bills I had – almost all of the money I had to take home to Kristie from the last ten days besides the check for the medical bill. As I counted out $140 into his hand, tears welled up in his eyes, and I felt the presence of God.

Slowly he dropped to one knee and put a hand to one suitcase clasp and then the other. Lifting the lid, he moved back so I could see the contents. It was full of Bibles! His wife opened the other suitcase; it was full of clothes, shoes and medicine. I dropped to my knees to join them, feeling the covers of the Bibles.

"I am a missionary with the Evangelical Church," he said, tears streaming down his cheeks.

"Where are you taking these?" I asked awed.

"To Guinea, Africa."

I was still sobbing when I called Kristie to tell her about what the Lord had done. "Why are you crying Chad? It's just a late flight . . ." Kristie said, confused, as I tried to talk through the tears.

"No, no, it's these missionaries. No, it's more than just that even." I told her the whole story about the suitcases. "See Kristie, it's about more than just my wanting to be generous; it's about obeying the prompting of the Holy Spirit in order to make sure I bless the people that are on His heart," I told her, explaining to myself more than to her.

"I understand now about the $1,300. God doesn't just want to bless us, He blesses us so we can be a blessing to others!"

CHAPTER 28

MIRACLES
AND
RESTORATION

The more I speak at assemblies, the more I realize that my story isn't an exception in today's culture, but more of the norm. Young people come to me all the time with stories so horrific I wonder how they have survived. Stories like the one from a petite, 14-year-old who came up to me after an assembly to ask how to get through the pain of having been raped by her older brother when she was seven, then tied to a chair while he sat in front of her and blew his head off, his brains literally spraying on her face and the blood and tissue covering her bound body.

Maybe you've read this book as one of those kids, hurting from a life of struggle and pain. The urgency of reaching kids like you burns within me, and I want you to know that if I made it, so can you.

My heart also goes out to the kids who have given in to the lies of satan that alcohol and drugs are the way to escape pain. I want you to receive this message of encouragement that it doesn't have to be that way. There is a purpose for your life. It may not seem that way now, but I can promise you this; if you just trust in Jesus, a few years from now you'll look back at your life and realize that there was a purpose for you. God is faithful, and he will direct you if you'll just surrender your life to him.

If you trust in God, you will not be alone. We see the fruit of our ministry when sixty to eighty percent of the kids we talk to in public school assemblies show up for the evening events, where we present without excuse Jesus Christ, His hope and His salvation. The response has been amazing. Thousands of young people are coming to Christ for the first time. These kids are being discipled and the vast majority are plugging into churches and sticking with their commitments. One church with a youth group of nearly two hundred swelled to over seven hundred kids and maintained those numbers by discipling and grounding each individual in the Word. Other churches all over the country are seeing similar, dramatic results.

This generation of young people is different than any other. They are searching for truth. They lie in bed at night and say "What's going to happen to me when I die." They're not looking for phony hype, they are searching; and what they are searching for is Jesus Christ. When they catch hold of the reality of who he is, there is no stopping them, they are unashamed. The passion of these new on-fire-for-God teens doesn't come from complicated formulas or programs, but the simplicity of a deep desire embedded in them to know the living God.

As I drove down the road, coming home from a speaking engagement recently, I glanced in the rearview mirror. I caught an expression of Kiersten's that made me think of Wendy. I offered up praises to the Lord for the way He's brought Wendy through all we experienced together. She's married and the mother of two precious girls herself now; she is an incredible mom.

I looked back at Cameron, and he asked me how long until

we'd be home so he could see Grandpa. I offered up more praises to the Lord for not only having given me the greatest father on earth, but the greatest grandpa for my children. Living with us and taking care of the house while we travel, Dad would be waiting to embrace Cameron and Kiersten as soon as we pulled in the drive.

Tears misted my sight as I watched the sweetness of my two children and realized they will never have to experience the family trauma I saw growing up. Jesus has truly given me peace in my family.

I reflected on the ups and downs in Mom's life, and I was flooded with the revelation that we serve a God of miracles. I've seen her lay dead for over seven minutes and come back to life. I've seen her lie in a corner and almost die from the withdrawals of cocaine as she fought her addictions. I marveled at how we found her in Atlanta when everything was against us. I remembered how I had to finally release her totally to God's care. If she was going to become truly freed from the bondages that enslaved her, it wasn't going to be because Chad was there to beat up some boyfriend. I finally put her in God's hands.

As I drove, the tears streamed down my cheeks because I finally have the peace I've always craved: my mom gave her life to Jesus! She's been saved for nearly five years now. She's had her struggles, but her life is committed to Christ, and I see the God of continuing miracles in her. More than that, God has been a God of restoration. She has been given the opportunity to genuinely enjoy children through her grandchildren, not only clean and sober, but with the joy of the Lord. She's taken back the ground satan stole from her and is singing praises for God once again like she used to do as a little girl. Best of all, Mom and I have an incredible relationship that has only been possible because of the empowering grace of God in our lives.

Maybe you've identified with my mom as you read this book, and you think your life is hopeless. You may be in a hotel room, separated from your kids and feeling condemned because your life is a mess because of drugs or alcohol. This book is here to tell you there is hope. It's not an accident that someone gave you this book and you've read this far; it's a divine appointment. Jesus loves you and has a plan and a purpose for your life. Maybe you don't know God and have never been in church, but you know there is a huge void in your life. If something is stirring within you, you need to keep reading. And, be sure to read my mom's specific encouragement for you at the end of this book.

Whoever you are or wherever you've been, if you find that as you read this book it stirs something inside of you and you have a desire to know God, you want that relationship with Christ, you can have it now. Living for Jesus Christ isn't as difficult as we make it sometimes. Every one of us has this in common: we make mistakes. Romans 3:23 says, "For all have sinned and fall short of the glory of God." The Bible is very clear: there is punishment for sin. Romans 6:23 says that "the wages of sin is death." The Bible is also very clear that there is only one way to heaven and it isn't by how many good things we do or how nice we are to people. It's not through Buddha or Muhammad, but Jesus Christ only. Acts 4:12 explains it this way, "Salvation is found in no one else, for there is no other name under heaven given to men by which we must be saved." You need to confess that openly as explained in Romans 10:9, "That if you confess with your mouth, 'Jesus is Lord,' and believe in your heart that God raised him from the dead, you will be saved."

If you want to receive Jesus Christ as your personal savior right now, pray this prayer with me: "Heavenly Father, I ask you right now, as I read this book, to come into my heart and be my best friend. Forgive me for all of my sins; I surrender my life to you, Jesus. When you died on the cross at Calvary, it was for me – today. I give my life fully to you. In Jesus name, amen."

If you prayed that prayer, welcome to the kingdom of God! Be sure you tell someone, perhaps a pastor or Christian friend, what you've done before you go to sleep tonight. I may never get to meet you in person, but we are going to spend eternity together! My mom wants to give you a message of encouragement as well; be sure to read her epilogue at the end of the book. You know, I didn't get to spend much of my childhood with my mom, but I get to spend eternity with her!

Know that when I travel from place to place bringing the message of hope and salvation that I don't just look back at my own family in the rearview mirror. I also look forward, deep into the bright blue horizon and pray for all the hurting people who haven't been reached yet, saying "Jesus, give them peace."

EPILOGUE

I left the book on the kitchen table for two days. I finally opened the package with more pain and fear than anyone could possibly imagine. The idea of my dreadful life of selfishness and child abuse, in full print for the whole world to read seemed more than I could bear. And then I found the note...

"Dear Mom, I know this is going to be difficult for you to read... but I want you to know that I love you with all my heart. What the enemy intended for evil, God has turned around for good. Thousands are coming to Jesus because of our story. I love you Mom... I love you." Your son, Chad.

I opened the book and began to read. Tears filled my eyes. Many of the stories were like a dream. I was in a black out most of the time, but soon I began to re-live and remember many of those horrible nights. The things I put my children through. The terrible selfish life I had led. And yet, here was my son saying, "Mom, it's okay... I love you, Mom."

What a precious son! What an awesome God! I wept bitterly. What a story of God's grace. It is hard to believe God could forgive someone as heartless as me. You see, no one realizes more than I, that I do not deserve his forgiveness. Believe me, I do not take it for granted. I do not understand how Christ can love and forgive me. I only know that in those lonely nights when I longed to be a good mother, those nights when I was strung out on drugs and alcohol…the same God that was listening to my little boy's cry…was hearing the cry of my heart, "God help me! God please set me free!" Jesus had a plan for my Chad's life, my Wendy's life, and yes, even mine.

Everyday, when I see little children, especially my grandchildren, with parents that watch their every move, never leaving their side, laughing at every little funny thing they do, staying up with them all night when they are sick, making a big deal of the first picture they drew and taking photos of the silliest little events in their lives, I think, "You lousy, rotten devil! Everything I could have been, everything my children could have had you tried to steal. But you didn't win. Jesus won! Today, my son could have a great name in the NBA with thousands of fans, but instead he's winning thousands of fans for Christ.

No, son. This book is not difficult for me. It is the greatest achievement in my life.

Ephesians 6:12 "For we wrestle not against flesh and blood, but against principalities, against powers, against the rulers of the darkness of this world, against spiritual wickedness in high places."

I love you my son,

Mom

Chad's mom and dad on their wedding day

Chad (8 months) and Wendy (2) pose for a picture

*Chad's mom and
dad with Wendy*

A rare Christmas together as a family

Chad and Wendy in the cold room

Chad and Wendy enjoying time with their dad and cousin Tim

Chad and Wendy preparing to go visit Mom in rehab

*Chad's 1st grade
school picture*

A Christmas without Mom

Chad's 11th birthday party without Mom

Chad's senior picture

Wendy's senior picture

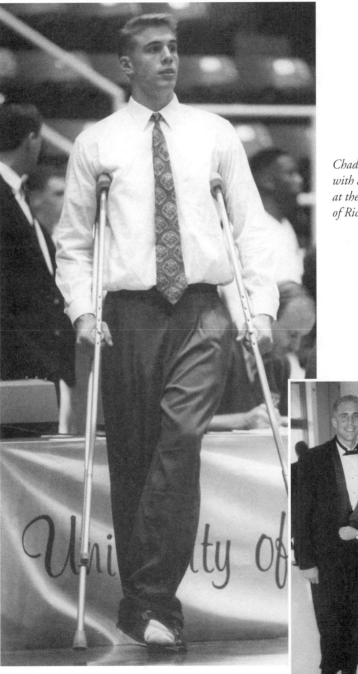

Chad sidelined with an injury at the University of Richmond

Chad and his beautiful wife Kristie at a friend's wedding

Chad, Kristie and Cameron before a game at the University of Pittsburgh

Cameron at nine months old...
Like father, like son!

Chad dunking on Seton Hall University in a Big East matchup at Fitzgerald Field House

Aunt Wendy comes for a visit

Chad with Kristie and his dad after a game at Pittsburgh

Chad with cousin and best friend, Tim Bach

Chad holding his MVP trophy after a game in Italy, playing for Team America

Chad dunking for Gijon Baloncesto his rookie season in Gijon, Spain

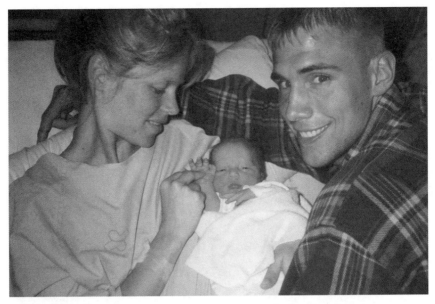

Chad and Kristie celebrating the birth of their precious little girl Kiersten

Cameron having fun with his new sister

Cameron posing with dad and sis' on his 4th birthday

Chad and family enjoying the sights in Tenerife, Spain

Kristie and Cameron enjoying whale-watching with Grandpa in Tenerife

Cameron and Kiersten clowning around on the balcony in Tenerife

Kiersten enjoying "Daddy Time"

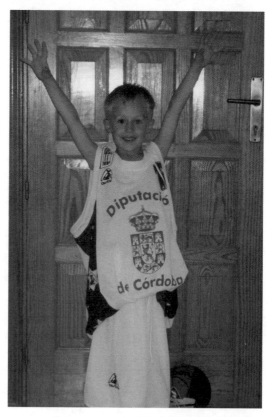

Cameron wearing his dad's All-Star uniform

Chad's mom Kathie being baptized in October, 2000 — What a miracle!

Grandma enjoying time with Kristie and the grandchildren

Grandma teaching Cameron how to play with a yo-yo

Chad and Kristie's two blessings… Cameron (6) and Kiersten (3)

*Cameron and Kiersten
enjoying Florida*

Chad motivating America's youth through high school assemblies

Chad inspiring teenagers at a high school football stadium in Georgia